FAMILY ISSUES IN THE 21ST CENTURY

SAME-SEX MARRIAGE BANS AND FEDERAL TAX ISSUES IN THE AFTERMATH OF UNITED STATES V. WINDSOR

FAMILY ISSUES IN THE 21ST CENTURY

Additional books in this series can be found on Nova's website under the Series tab.

Additional e-books in this series can be found on Nova's website under the e-book tab.

FAMILY ISSUES IN THE 21ST CENTURY

SAME-SEX MARRIAGE BANS AND FEDERAL TAX ISSUES IN THE AFTERMATH OF UNITED STATES V. WINDSOR

MAXINE DUNN
EDITOR

NOVINKA
New York

For permission to use material from this book please contact us:
Telephone 631-231-7269; Fax 631-231-8175
Web Site: http://www.novapublishers.com

Additional color graphics may be available in the e-book version of this book.

Library of Congress Cataloging-in-Publication Data

ISBN: 978-1-63463-844-9

Published by Nova Science Publishers, Inc. † New York

CONTENTS

PREFACE

The recognition of same-sex marriage generates debate on both the federal and state levels. Either legislatively or judicially, same-sex marriage is legal in more than a dozen states and the District of Columbia. Conversely, many states have statutory or constitutional prohibitions against same-sex marriage. Courts are beginning to address the constitutionality of these "defense of marriage" laws using equal protection and due process analysis. In *United States v. Windsor*, the U.S. Supreme Court struck down the federal ban on benefits for legally married same-sex couples. However, the Court indicated that it was taking no position on a state's authority to forbid same-sex marriages. Lower courts have interpreted *Windsor* broadly and have found such bans to violate equal protection and due process principles. This book discusses same-sex marriage bans and federal tax issues in the aftermath of *United Sates v. Windsor.*

Chapter 1 – The issue of same-sex marriage generates debate on both the federal and state levels. Either legislatively or judicially, same-sex marriage is legal in more than a dozen states. Conversely, many states have statutes and/or constitutional amendments limiting marriage to the union of one man and one woman. These state-level variations raise questions about the validity of such unions outside the contracted jurisdiction and have bearing on the distribution of state and/or federal benefits. As federal agencies grappled with the interplay of the Defense of Marriage Act (DOMA) and the distribution of federal marriage-based benefits, questions arose regarding DOMA's constitutionality and the appropriate standard (strict, intermediate, or rational basis) of review to apply to the statute. In *United States v. Windsor*, a closely divided U.S. Supreme Court held that Section 3 of DOMA, which prohibited federal recognition of same-sex marriage, violated due process and equal protection principles. As such, federal statutes that refer to a marriage and/or spouse for federal purposes should be interpreted as applying equally to legally married same-sex couples recognized by the state. However, the Court left unanswered questions such as (1) whether same-sex couples have a fundamental right to marry and (2) whether state bans on same-sex marriage are constitutionally permissible. In the aftermath of the *Windsor* decision, lower federal courts have begun to address the constitutionality of state statutory and constitutional bans on same-sex marriage. To date, appellate courts in the Fourth, Seventh, Ninth and Tenth Circuits have upheld lower courts' decisions striking down such bans. The Fourth and Tenth Circuit Courts have concluded that the bans in three states (Utah, Oklahoma, and Virginia) violate both the equal protection and due process guarantees of the Fourteenth Amendment by impermissibly infringing on the fundamental right to marry. Relying on a series of "marriage" cases, these courts have taken a broad or expansive view of the fundamental right to marry and found that this right encompasses same-sex marriage and the recognition of these unions across state lines. While district courts were split as to the appropriate level of judicial review, both appellate courts concluded that strict scrutiny is appropriate as a fundamental right is implicated. Although arriving at the same result as its sister circuits—striking down same-sex marriage bans (Indiana, Wisconsin, Idaho and Nevada)—the Seventh and Ninth Circuits took a different approach. They declined to address the issue of whether the fundamental right to marry encompasses same-sex unions. Instead, they limited their analysis to the equal protection challenge. The courts concluded that discrimination based on sexual orientation warrants heightened scrutiny and that the states' proffered justifications failed to further any legitimate purpose. Appeals are pending in other circuits. The Sixth Circuit held oral arguments concerning the constitutionality of four states' (Kentucky, Michigan, Ohio, and Tennessee) bans. Some commentators believe that there is a possibility that the Sixth Circuit may uphold one or more of these bans. Recently, the Supreme Court denied review of petitions from the Fourth, Seventh, and Tenth Circuits (covering Indiana, Oklahoma, Utah, Virginia, and Wisconsin). It remains uncertain whether the U.S. Supreme Court will decline to intervene until a circuit split occurs.

Chapter 2 – This report will provide an overview of the potential federal tax implications for same-sex married couples of the U.S. Supreme Court ruling in *United States v. Windsor*, with a focus on the federal income tax. Estate tax issues are also discussed. Importantly, this report focuses on changes in the *interpretation and administration* of federal tax law resulting from the Court's decision. The decision itself did not amend federal tax law.

This report is not intended to address *all* tax-related issues that may arise as a result of the *Windsor* decision. Such discussion is beyond the scope of this report.

Chapter 3 – Report of the U.S. Supreme Court, on Decision of the Supreme Court of the United States in the Case of United States v. Windsor, Executor of the Estate of Spyer, et al. dated June 26, 2013.

In: Same-Sex Marriage Bans …
Editor: Maxine Dunn

ISBN: 978-1-63463-844-9

Chapter 1

SAME-SEX MARRIAGE: A LEGAL BACKGROUND AFTER *UNITED STATES V. WINDSOR*[*]

Alison M. Smith

SUMMARY

The issue of same-sex marriage generates debate on both the federal and state levels. Either legislatively or judicially, same-sex marriage is legal in more than a dozen states. Conversely, many states have statutes and/or constitutional amendments limiting marriage to the union of one man and one woman. These state-level variations raise questions about the validity of such unions outside the contracted jurisdiction and have bearing on the distribution of state and/or federal benefits. As federal agencies grappled with the interplay of the Defense of Marriage Act (DOMA) and the distribution of federal marriage-based benefits, questions arose regarding DOMA's constitutionality and the appropriate standard (strict, intermediate, or rational basis) of review to apply to the statute.

In *United States v. Windsor*, a closely divided U.S. Supreme Court held that Section 3 of DOMA, which prohibited federal recognition of same-sex marriage, violated due process and equal protection principles.

---

[*] This is an edited, reformatted and augmented version of a Congressional Research Service publication R43481, prepared for Members and Committees of Congress, dated October 10, 2014.

As such, federal statutes that refer to a marriage and/or spouse for federal purposes should be interpreted as applying equally to legally married same-sex couples recognized by the state. However, the Court left unanswered questions such as (1) whether same-sex couples have a fundamental right to marry and (2) whether state bans on same-sex marriage are constitutionally permissible.

In the aftermath of the *Windsor* decision, lower federal courts have begun to address the constitutionality of state statutory and constitutional bans on same-sex marriage. To date, appellate courts in the Fourth, Seventh, Ninth and Tenth Circuits have upheld lower courts' decisions striking down such bans. The Fourth and Tenth Circuit Courts have concluded that the bans in three states (Utah, Oklahoma, and Virginia) violate both the equal protection and due process guarantees of the Fourteenth Amendment by impermissibly infringing on the fundamental right to marry. Relying on a series of "marriage" cases, these courts have taken a broad or expansive view of the fundamental right to marry and found that this right encompasses same-sex marriage and the recognition of these unions across state lines. While district courts were split as to the appropriate level of judicial review, both appellate courts concluded that strict scrutiny is appropriate as a fundamental right is implicated.

Although arriving at the same result as its sister circuits—striking down same-sex marriage bans (Indiana, Wisconsin, Idaho and Nevada)—the Seventh and Ninth Circuits took a different approach. They declined to address the issue of whether the fundamental right to marry encompasses same-sex unions. Instead, they limited their analysis to the equal protection challenge. The courts concluded that discrimination based on sexual orientation warrants heightened scrutiny and that the states' proffered justifications failed to further any legitimate purpose.

Appeals are pending in other circuits. The Sixth Circuit held oral arguments concerning the constitutionality of four states' (Kentucky, Michigan, Ohio, and Tennessee) bans. Some commentators believe that there is a possibility that the Sixth Circuit may uphold one or more of these bans. Recently, the Supreme Court denied review of petitions from the Fourth, Seventh, and Tenth Circuits (covering Indiana, Oklahoma, Utah, Virginia, and Wisconsin). It remains uncertain whether the U.S. Supreme Court will decline to intervene until a circuit split occurs.

INTRODUCTION

The recognition of same-sex marriage generates debate on both the federal and state levels. Either legislatively or judicially, same-sex marriage is legal in more than a dozen states and the District of Columbia.[1] Conversely, many states have statutory[2] or constitutional prohibitions[3] against same-sex marriage. Courts are beginning to address the constitutionality of these "defense of marriage" laws using equal protection and due process analysis. In *United States v. Windsor*,[4] the U.S. Supreme Court struck down the federal ban on benefits for legally married same-sex couples. However, the Court indicated that it was taking no position on a state's authority to forbid same-sex marriages. Lower courts have interpreted *Windsor* broadly and have found such bans to violate equal protection and due process principles.

GENERAL CONSTITUTIONAL PRINCIPLES

Equal Protection[5]

The Fourteenth Amendment provides, in relevant part, that "[n]o State shall ... deny to any person within its jurisdiction the equal protection of the laws."[6] Under the Supreme Court's equal protection jurisprudence, "the general rule is that legislation is presumed to be valid and will be sustained if the classification drawn by the statute is rationally related to a legitimate state interest."[7] Laws based on suspect classifications such as race or gender, however, typically receive heightened scrutiny and require a stronger, if not compelling, state interest to justify the classification.

Traditionally, courts have not considered sexual orientation to be a suspect category. In theory, therefore, the government need only advance a rational basis for enacting a statute that treats individuals differently depending on their sexual orientation. However, Supreme Court and recent lower court rulings have raised questions about whether classifications involving sexual orientation can meet this most deferential standard of review.

For example, in *Romer v. Evans*, the Court held that Amendment 2 of the Colorado constitution, which barred localities from enacting civil rights protections on the basis of sexual orientation, violated the Equal Protection Clause.[8] According to the Court, the Colorado amendment violated the guarantee of equal protection because the law was motivated strictly by animus and because there was otherwise no rational basis for enacting such a sweeping restriction on the legal rights of gays and lesbians.[9]

Substantive due Process (Right to Privacy)

The Fourteenth Amendment's Due Process Clause has a substantive component which "provides heightened protection against government interference with certain fundamental rights and liberty interests."[10] Although the Constitution does not specifically mention a fundamental right to privacy, courts recognize this right to encompass interpersonal relations.[11] For example, in *Lawrence v. Texas*,[12] the Court considered a constitutional challenge to a Texas statute that made it a crime for individuals to engage in homosexual sodomy. The Court held that the Fourteenth Amendment's due process privacy protections encompass private, consensual gay sex.[13]

While states have the authority to regulate marriage, this authority is not without limits. In a series of cases, the Court has struck down laws that impermissibly burden an individual's ability to exercise the right to marry.[14] For example, in *Loving v. Virginia*[15] the Court found that Virginia's anti-miscegenation statute violated both the Equal Protection Clause and Due Process Clause of the Fourteenth Amendment. The Court held that individuals could not be restricted from exercising their existing right to marry on account of the race of their chosen partner.[16] According to the Court,

> Marriage is one of the "basic civil rights of man," fundamental to our very existence and survival ... To deny this fundamental freedom on so unsupportable a basis as the racial classifications embodied in these statutes, classifications so directly subversive of the principle of equality at the heart of the Fourteenth Amendment, is surely to deprive all the State's citizens of liberty without due process of law. The Fourteenth Amendment requires that the freedom of choice to marry may not be restricted by invidious racial discrimination. Under our Constitution, the freedom to marry, or not marry, a person of another race resides with the individual and cannot be infringed by the State.

United States v. Windsor: The Challenge to the Federal Defense of Marriage Act

In *United States v. Windsor*,[17] a closely divided Court struck down a portion of the federal Defense of Marriage Act (DOMA),[18] finding that it violated the equal protection guarantees of the Fifth Amendment. DOMA was enacted "[t]o define and protect the institution of marriage." Section 2[19] allows all states, territories, possessions, and Indian tribes to refuse to recognize an act of any other jurisdiction that designates a relationship between individuals of the same sex as a marriage.[20] Section 3 had required that, for purposes of federal enactments, marriage would be defined as the union of one man and one woman.[21] As federal agencies grappled with the interplay of DOMA and the distribution of federal marriage-based benefits, questions arose regarding DOMA's constitutionality and the appropriate standard (strict, intermediate, or rational basis) of review to be applied to the statute.

In *Windsor*, the plaintiff and her late spouse were New York residents who had been legally married in Canada and whose same-sex marriage was legally recognized in New York. Because of DOMA, the decedent's estate could not claim the unlimited marital deduction for purposes of the federal estate tax. As a result, the estate owed $363,053 in taxes, which were paid. Ms. Windsor sued, claiming that Section 3 of DOMA violated the equal protection clause of the U.S. Constitution. Using a deferential rational basis review and ordering a refund of the taxes paid, the district court granted the plaintiff's motion for summary judgment holding that DOMA's definitional section was unconstitutional.[22] The lower court's ruling was affirmed on appeal; however, the appellate court determined that intermediate scrutiny was the appropriate level of review to apply to the provision.

In an opinion authored by Justice Kennedy, the Supreme Court relied on federalism, due process, and equal protection principles. The Court declined to determine whether Section 3 of DOMA is an unconstitutional "intrusion on state power." Instead the Court struck down the section on equal protection grounds using a "closer examination" and rational basis analysis.

In its opinion, the Court examined the historical relationship between the federal and state governments concerning domestic relations. Traditionally, states have maintained exclusive control over defining and regulating marriage. While marriage laws may vary among the states, marriages within a state are treated equally. According to the Court, Section 3 of DOMA runs contrary to this practice. Specifically, the Court noted that "[b]y creating two contradictory marriage regimes within the same State, DOMA forces same-sex couples to live as married for the purpose of state law but unmarried for the purpose of federal law, thus diminishing the stability and predictability of basic personal relations the State has found it proper to acknowledge and protect."[23]

After examining DOMA's history, the Court concluded that "its purpose is to discourage enactment of state same-sex marriage laws and to restrict the freedom and choice of couples married ... "[24] As such, the Court found Section

3 invalid, specifically stating that "no legitimate purpose overcomes the purpose and effect to disparage and to injure those whom the State, by its marriage laws, sought to protect in personhood and dignity."[25]

In their respective dissents, Chief Justice Roberts emphasized that the majority opinion only applied to actual marriages;[26] Justice Scalia speculated that the decision would lead to a constitutional right to same-sex marriage;[27] and Justice Alito argued that there is no constitutional right for same-sex couples to marry.[28]

While the Court resolved the question of the constitutionality of a federal definition of marriage excluding same-sex couples, it left unresolved several questions: (1) whether same-sex couples have a fundamental right to marry; (2) whether sexual orientation classifications warrant heightened scrutiny or the more deferential rational basis standard of review; (3) whether a state may prohibit same-sex marriages within its borders; and (4) whether a state may refuse to recognize a same-sex marriage validly contracted outside its borders.

POST-*WINDSOR* LITIGATION

In the aftermath of the *Windsor* decision, lower federal courts have begun to address the constitutionality of state statutory and constitutional bans on same-sex marriage and recognition of such unions.[29] To date, federal appellate courts in the Fourth,[30] Seventh,[31] and Tenth[32] Circuits as well as several federal district courts[33] have broadly construed *Windsor* and struck down state provisions which prohibit same-sex marriages within their borders. In *Kitchen v. Herbert*,[34] *Bishop v. Smith*,[35] and *Bostic v. Schaefer*,[36] both appellate courts affirmed lower court decisions which found that such bans violate both the equal protection and due process guarantees of the Fourteenth Amendment as they impermissibly infringe on the fundamental right to marry. In *Kitchen*, the court concluded that "a state may not deny the issuance of a marriage license to two persons, or refuse to recognize their marriage, based solely upon the sex of the persons in the marriage union."[37] Relying on a series of "marriage" cases, the appellate courts have taken an expansive view of the fundamental right to marry and found that the right encompasses same-sex unions and the recognition of these unions. While most district courts have used a rational basis review, both appellate courts concluded that strict scrutiny is appropriate as a fundamental right is implicated. Conversely, a federal district court upheld Louisiana's prohibition and nonrecognition of same-sex marriage against equal protection and due process challenges. [38]

According to the appellate courts, the fundamental right to marry includes the right to choose a same-sex partner and have that union recognized across state lines.[39] The courts relied on a series of cases in which the Supreme Court struck down laws that prohibited interracial marriage,[40] marriage of individuals owing child support,[41] and marriage of prison inmates.[42] Both circuit courts have determined that these cases demonstrate a broad right to marry "not circumscribed based on the characteristics of the individuals seeking to exercise that right."[43] The courts noted that the *Loving* Court did not create a new right to interracial marriage, but instead considered it to be a subset of "marriage." Accordingly, it follows that same-sex marriage is similarly included within the fundamental right to marry. According to the Fourth Circuit, these cases support the notion that the right to marry is a matter of an individual's freedom of choice.[44]

Both appellate courts applied strict scrutiny as the standard of review for equal protection and due process analysis, which requires the state to demonstrate that its classification is narrowly tailored to serve a compelling interest.[45] The states advanced several justifications including responsible procreation, optimal child-rearing, and civil strife. The courts rejected the states' justifications as they were mostly predicated on a link between marriage and procreation.[46] In essence, the court found the bans under inclusive as procreation is not a prerequisite to marriage for opposite-sex couples. As to the "civic strife" justification, the court in *Kitchen* noted that Supreme Court precedent has "repeatedly held that public opposition cannot provide cover for a violation of fundamental rights."[47] For these reasons, the appellate courts found that the bans violated both the equal protection and due process guarantees of the Fourteenth Amendment.

While the Seventh Circuit also struck down same-sex marriage bans before it in *Baskin v. Bogan*,[48] it took a different approach. The court declined to address the due process challenge and whether the fundamental right to marry encompasses same-sex unions. Instead, it focused on the equal protection challenge. In determining the appropriate level of review, the court found that "homosexuals are among the most stigmatized, misunderstood, and discriminated against minorities...."[49] Therefore, the court concluded that those individuals who seek to enter into a same-sex marriage are part of a quasi-suspect class requiring the government to advance a sufficiently persuasive justification for discrimination. The court found unpersuasive the proffered reasons for the bans: child welfare, preservation of traditional marriage, and procreation.[50] Moreover, the court noted that the "discrimination against same-sex couples is irrational, and therefore unconstitutional even if the discrimination is not subjected to heightened scrutiny...."[51]

IMPLICATIONS

A state's recognition of same-sex marriage implicates a myriad of benefits, rights, and responsibilities on both the federal and state levels. For example, for federal programs under the Social Security Administration's (SSA's) purview (Social Security, Medicare, and Supplemental Security Income), the agency generally defers to a state's definition of marriage. SSA guidance now allows for the payment of Social Security spousal benefits when the number holder (1) was married in a state that permits same-sex marriage; and (2) is domiciled (at the time of application, or while the claim is pending a final determination) in a state that recognizes same-sex marriage. On the state level, there may be tax implications as same-sex couples would be able to file a joint state tax return to match their federal return,[52] as well as implications for the holding, transfer, and inheritance of property.

CONCLUSION

The Supreme Court has not expressly resolved the issue of the constitutionality of state prohibitions or non-recognition of same-sex marriages. However, rulings in *Loving*, *Romer*, *Lawrence*, and *Windsor* appear to call into question the constitutionality of such prohibitions. Collectively, these cases prohibit states from passing laws based on animus toward gays and lesbians, extend constitutional protection to sexual choices of homosexuals, and prohibit the federal government from treating opposite-sex and same-sex marriages differently. Lower federal courts that have addressed the issue of state prohibitions on same-sex marriage have unanimously concluded that such bans violate equal protection and due process principles. While these courts recognize a state's power to regulate marriage, such regulation must comport with an individual's constitutional rights. These courts have rejected states' asserted governmental interests and instead found them not rationally related to the states' prohibitions of same-sex marriage. Two appellate courts have broadly interpreted the fundamental right to marriage to encompass same-sex marriages and the recognition of such unions. These courts concluded that the right to marry is a matter of an individual's freedom of choice. Rulings requiring states to recognize same-sex marriages entered in other states would apparently supercede and call into question the validity of Section 2 of DOMA, which permits the non-recognition of such unions. Additional rulings from the courts, including the Supreme Court, may be forthcoming before the validity of these state bans is definitively resolved.

End Notes

[1] California, Connecticut, Colorado, Delaware, Hawaii, Illinois, Iowa, Maine, Maryland, Massachusetts, Minnesota, New Hampshire, New Jersey, New Mexico, New York, Rhode Island, Vermont, and Washington.

[2] Indiana, Pennsylvania, West Virginia, and Wyoming.

[3] Alabama, Alaska, Arizona, Arkansas, Colorado, Florida, Georgia, Idaho, Kansas, Kentucky, Louisiana, Michigan, Missouri, Montana, Nebraska, Nevada, North Carolina, North Dakota, Ohio, Oklahoma, Oregon, South Carolina, South Dakota, Tennessee, Texas, Utah, Virginia, and Wisconsin.

[4] 133 S.Ct. 2675 (2013).

[5] The Fifth Amendment applies to the federal government while the Fourteenth Amendment applies to the states. In Bolling v. Sharpe (347 U.S. 497 [1954]), the Supreme Court interpreted the Fifth Amendment's Due Process Clause to include an equal protection element. In Buckley v. Valeo (424 U.S. 1, 93 [1976]), the Court stated that "[e]qual protection analysis in the Fifth Amendment area, is the same as that under the Fourteenth Amendment."

[6] U.S. Const. amend. XIV, §1.

[7] City of Cleburne v. Cleburne Living Center, 473 U.S. 432, 440 (1985).

[8] 517 U.S. 620, 635 (1996).

[9] Id. at 634.

[10] Washington v. Glucksberg, 521 U.S. 702, 720 (1997).

[11] Loving v. Virginia, 338 U.S. 1 (1967). In addition to the freedoms explicitly protected by the Bill of Rights, the "liberty" specifically protected by the Due Process Clause includes the right to have children, Skinner v. Oklahoma ex rel. Williamson, 316 U.S. 535 (1942); to direct the education and upbringing of one's children, Meyer v. Nebraska, 262 U.S. 390 (1923); Pierce v. Society of Sisters, 268 U.S. 510 (1925); to marital privacy, Griswold v. Connecticut, 381 U.S. 479 (1965); to use contraception, id.; Eisenstadt v. Baird, 405 U.S. 438 (1972); to bodily integrity, Rochin v. California, 342 U.S. 165 (1952); and to abortion, Planned Parenthood of Southeastern Pa. v. Casey, 505 U.S. 833 (1992).

[12] 539 U.S. 558 (2003).

[13] Id. at 578 stating that:

The petitioners are entitled to respect for their private lives. The State cannot demean or control their destiny by making their private sexual conduct a crime. The right to liberty under the Due Process Clause gives them the full right to engage in their conduct without the intervention of the government. It is a promise of the Constitution that there is a realm of personal liberty which the government cannot enter. The Texas statute furthers no legitimate state interest which can justify its intrusion into the personal and private life of the individual.

[14] See e.g., Zablocki v. Redhail, 434 U.S. 347 (1978) (invalidating a Wisconsin statute that required any Wisconsin resident to prove compliance with any support obligation for non-custodial children); Turner v. Safley, 482 U.S. 78 (1987)(invalidating a Missouri regulation that prohibited inmates from marrying unless the prison superintendent approved of the marriage).

[15] 388 U.S. 1 (1967).

[16] Id. at 12.

[17] 133 S.Ct. at 2696. Section 2 was not challenged.

[18] P.L. 104-199, 110 Stat. 2419 (codified at 1 U.S.C. §7 and 28 U.S.C. §1738C).

[19] 28 U.S.C. §1738C states:

No State, territory, or possession of the United States, or Indian tribe, shall be required to give effect to any public act, record, or judicial proceeding of any other State, territory, possession, or tribe respecting a relationship between persons of the same sex that is treated as a marriage under the laws of such other State, territory, possession, or tribe, or a right or claim arising from such relationship.

[20] Section 2 was not challenged in Windsor.

[21] 1 U.S.C. §7 stated:

In determining the meaning of any Act of Congress, or of any ruling, regulation, or interpretation of the various administrative bureaus and agencies of the United States, the word "marriage" means only a legal union between one man and one woman as husband and wife, and the word "spouse" refers only to a person of the opposite sex who is a husband or a wife.

[22] Windsor v. United States, No. 10 Civ. 8435 (S.D.N.Y. June 6, 2012).

[23] 133 S.Ct. at 2694.

[24] Id. at 2693.

[25] Id. at 2696.

[26] Id. at 2696 (Chief Justice Roberts, dissenting)(stating that [t]he Court does not have before it, and the logic of its opinion does not decide, the distinct question whether the States, in the exercise of their "historic and essential authority to define the marital relation," ante, at 2692," may continue to utilize the traditional definition of marriage.").

[27] Id. at 2710 (Scalia, J., dissenting)(explaining that "the majority arms well every challenger to a state law restricting marriage to its traditional definition" and transposing certain portions of the majority opinion to reveal how it could assist these challengers).

[28] Id. at 2714 (Alito, J., dissenting)(stating that "[w]hat Windsor and the United States seek, therefore, is not the protection of a deeply rooted right but the recognition of a very new right, and they seek this innovation not from a legislative body elected by the people, but from unelected judges.").

[29] Kitchen v. Herbert, No. 13-4178, 2014 WL 2868044, *1, *16 (C.A. 10 (Utah)) (stating "we agree with the multiple district courts that have held that the fundamental right to marry necessarily includes the right to remain married.").

[30] Bostic v. Schaefer, Nos. 14-1167, 14-1169, 14-1173, 2014 WL 3702493 (C.A.4 (Va.)), *1, *13.

[31] Baskin v. Brogan, Nos. 14-2386, 14-2387, 14-2388, 14-2526, 2014 WL 4359059 (C.A.7 (Ind.)), *1 (covering challenges to Indiana and Wisconsin bans).

[32] Kitchen v. Herbert, No. 13-4178, 2014 WL 2868044, *1, *16 (C.A. 10 (Utah)); Bishop v. Smith, Nos. 14-5003, 14- 5006, 2014 WL 3537847 (C.A. 10 (Okla.)).

[33] Kitchen v. Herbert, No. 2:13-cv-217, 2013 WL 6697874, at *1 (D. Utah, December 23, 2013); Bishop v. Holder, No. 04-CV-848-TCK-TLW, 2014 WL 116013, at *1 (N.D. Okla., January 14, 2014); Bostic v. Rainey, Civil No. 2:13cv 395, 2014 WL 561978, at *1 (E.D. Va., February 13, 2014); Deboer v. Snyder, No. 12-CV-10285, 2014 WL 1100794, at *1 (E.D. Mich., March 21, 2014); Latta v. Otter, 2014 WL 1909999, at *1 (D. Idaho 2014); Geiger v. Kitzhaber, 2014 WL 2054264, at *1 (D. Or. May 19, 2014); Wolf v. Walker, 2014 WL 2558444 (W.D. Wis., June 6, 2014); De Leon v. Perry, 975 F.Supp.2d 632 (W.D. Tex., 2014).

[34] No. 13-4178, 2014 WL 2868044, *1, *1 (C.A. 10 (Utah)).

[35] Nos. 14-5003, 14-5006, 2014 WL 3537847 (C.A. 10 (Okla.)).

[36] Nos. 14-1167, 14-1169, 14-1173, 2014 WL 3702493 (C.A.4 (Va.)).

[37] Kitchen v. Herbert, No. 13-4178, 2014 WL 2868044, *1, *1 (C.A. 10 (Utah)); see also, Bostic v. Schaefer, Nos. 14- 1167, 14-1169, 14-1173, 2014 WL 3702493 (C.A.4 (Va.)), *1, *1; Bishop v. Smith, Nos. 14-5003, 14-5006, 2014 WL 3537847 (C.A. 10 (Okla.)).

[38] Robicheaux v. Caldwell, Nos. 13-5090, 14-97, 14-327, 2014 WL 4347099, *1, *1 (E.D. La. September 3, 2014).

[39] CF, Borman v. Plyes-Borman, No.2014CV36 located at http://sblog.s3.amazonaws.com/wp-content/uploads/2014/ 08/complete-copy-Tennessee-ruling.pdf (last visited August 14, 2014). Tennessee state court finding that the state's Anti-Recognition Law does not violate equal protection using a rational basis analysis.

[40] Loving v. Virginia, 388 U.S. 1 (1967).

[41] Zablocki v. Redhail, 434 U.S. 347 (1978)(invalidating a Wisconsin statute requiring any Wisconsin resident to prove compliance with any support obligation for non-custodial children).

[42] Turner v. Safley, 482 U.S. 78 (1987)(invalidating a Missouri regulation prohibiting inmates from marrying without the prison superintendent's approval).

[43] Bostic v. Schaefer, Nos. 14-1167, 14-1169, 14-1173, 2014 WL 3702493 (C.A.4 (Va.)), *1, *13.

[44] CF, Robicheaux v. Caldwell, Nos. 13-5090, 14-97, 14-327, 2014 WL 4347099, *1, fn 13 (E.D. La. September 3, 2014)(distinguishing listed cases).

[45] Id. at *6 - *8 (E.D. La. September 3, 2014)(upholding Louisiana's prohibition and non-recognition of same-sex marriage using a rational basis analysis as the relevant provisions do not implicate the fundamental right to marry).

[46] Id. at *8 (stating that "Louisiana has a legitimate interest...whether obsolete in the opinion of some, or not, in the opinion of other ... in linking children to an intact family formed by their two biological parents, as specifically underscored by Justice Kennedy in Windsor.").

[47] Kitchen v. Herbert, 2014 WL 2868044, at *30.

[48] Nos. 14-2386, 14-2387, 14-2388, 14-2526, 2014 WL 4359059 (C.A.7 (Ind.)), *1 (covering challenges to Indiana and Wisconsin bans).

[49] Id at*1, *5.

[50] Id. (stating that "[t]he challenged laws discriminate against a minority defined by an immutable characteristic, and the only rationale that the states put forth with any conviction—that same-sex couples and their children don't need marriage because same-sex couples can't produce children, intended or unintended—is so full of holes that it cannot be taken seriously."); see also, Latta v. Otter, No. 14-35420, 2014 WL 4977682, *1, *1 (C.A. 9 (Idaho)) (finding that states' (Idaho and Nevada) bans on same-sex marriage fail to further

any legitimate purpose, unjustifiably discriminate on the basis of sexual orientation, and are in violation of the Equal Protection Clause).

[51] Id.

[52] CRS Report R43157, The Potential Federal Tax Implications of United States v. Windsor (Striking Section 3 of the Defense of Marriage Act (DOMA)): Selected Issues, by Margot L. Crandall-Hollick, Molly F. Sherlock, and Carol A. Pettit.

In: Same-Sex Marriage Bans ...
Editor: Maxine Dunn
ISBN: 978-1-63463-844-9

Chapter 2

THE POTENTIAL FEDERAL TAX IMPLICATIONS OF *UNITED STATES V. WINDSOR* (STRIKING SECTION 3 OF THE DEFENSE OF MARRIAGE ACT (DOMA)): SELECTED ISSUES*

Margot L. Crandall-Hollick, Molly F. Sherlock and Carol A. Pettit

SCOPE OF THE REPORT

This report will provide an overview of the potential federal tax implications for same-sex married couples of the U.S. Supreme Court ruling in *United States v. Windsor*, with a focus on the federal income tax.[1] Estate tax issues are also discussed.[2] Importantly, this report focuses on changes in the *interpretation and administration* of federal tax law resulting from the Court's decision. The decision itself did not amend federal tax law. This report is not intended to address *all* tax-related issues that may arise as a result of the *Windsor* decision. Such discussion is beyond the scope of this report.

---

* This is an edited, reformatted and augmented version of a Congressional Research Service publication, CRS Report for Congress R43157, prepared for Members and Committees of Congress, from www.crs.gov, dated September 9, 2013.

UNITED STATES V. WINDSOR

On June 26, 2013, the U.S. Supreme Court held that Section 3[3] of the Defense of Marriage Act (DOMA)[4] is unconstitutional. Section 3 requires that, for purposes of federal enactments, marriage is limited to the union of one man and one woman and the word spouse is defined as someone of the opposite-sex who is a husband or wife.[5] Hence, prior to the *Windsor* decision, same-sex marriages were not recognized by the federal government for the receipt of federal benefits or for federal tax purposes. The Government Accountability Office (GAO) estimated in 2004 (the most recent estimates available) that there were 1,138 statutory provisions in the U.S. Code in which marital status was a factor in determining benefits.[6] Of these, almost 200 were statutory provisions of the Internal Revenue Code (IRC).[7]

SAME-SEX MARRIAGE RECOGNITION AND THE INTERNAL REVENUE CODE (IRC)

On August 29, 2013, the Department of the Treasury and Internal Revenue Service (IRS) ruled that all legal same-sex marriages will be recognized for federal tax purposes.[8] The ruling applies regardless of whether the couple resides in a state or jurisdiction that recognizes same-sex marriage.[9,] Thus, for federal tax purposes, same-sex couples who were legally married in one state, but reside in a state that does not recognize the marriage, will be treated as married.[10] The ruling does not apply to civil unions, registered domestic partnerships, or other formal relationships not denominated as a marriage under state law.[11]

Among same-sex couples who identify as married, more than half (56% or approximately 94,000 couples) reside in states that do not recognize same-sex marriage.[12] While the August 29, 2013, ruling provides certainty regarding federal tax filing status for these couples, the ruling may complicate tax filing at the state level.

There are 24 states that do not recognize same-sex marriage but do require taxpayers to reference federal tax returns in the process of preparing state tax returns.[13]

TAX ISSUES

With respect to federal tax-related issues, the ruling on Section 3 of DOMA will primarily affect married same-sex couples' federal income taxes. For the limited number of married same-sex individuals who have sufficient assets to be subject to the estate tax, potential estate tax liability may also be affected. Treating same-sex couples as married for federal tax purposes could have substantial financial implications for some affected couples. The budgetary impact from the perspective of the federal government, however, is likely small.[14] Currently, the U.S. Census Bureau estimates that there are 605,472 same-sex couples in the United States (less than one-half of one percent of all tax returns filed), of which approximately 168,000 (27.8%) self-identify as married.[15] It is not known whether all who self-identified as married were legally married in a jurisdiction recognizing same-sex marriage.[16]

Estate Tax

The unlimited marital deduction under the estate tax was at issue in *Windsor*.[17] Under current law, a deceased spouse's estate can transfer all of assets to the surviving spouse without incurring any estate tax.[18] Prior to the decision in *Windsor*, a married same-sex couple was not eligible for this spousal tax exemption. (The exemption amount is the amount of the estate which, when bequeathed to an heir, is tax-free. If the heir is a spouse, the exemption amount is unlimited.) Thus, for some couples, the *Windsor* decision could result in a reduced estate tax liability.[19]

In addition to being eligible for unlimited spousal transfers, same-sex couples may also benefit from transferability of exemption amounts to non-spouse beneficiaries. Unlike the unlimited spousal exemption, there is a limit on the amount of an estate which can pass to a non-spouse heir tax-free. As enacted, the estate tax is structured so that the first $5 million per individual or $10 million per federally recognized married couple (adjusted for inflation) of the estate and intervivos gifts (gifts made prior to death) are exempt from federal taxes when bequeathed to non-spouse beneficiaries, like children or non-relatives.[20]

In 2013, once adjusted for inflation, the exemption amount per individual is $5.25 million. Since any unused exemption amounts are transferable between spouses, if one spouse leaves an estate of $3 million upon death in

2013 to a non-spouse beneficiary, the remaining $2.25 of that deceased spouse's exemption amount would be transferred to the surviving spouse.[21] Hence, the surviving spouse's exemption amount would increase from $5.25 million (or, the amount of the exemption in the year the second spouse dies) to $7.5 million. Prior to the *Windsor* decision, the surviving same-sex spouse could only use his or her own exemption amount to make a tax-free bequest to a non-spouse beneficiary ($5.25 million in 2013). Hence, the surviving spouse of a same-sex marriage may, as a result of the *Windsor* decision, be able to bequeath a greater amount tax-free to a non-spouse beneficiary.

While the estate tax may have been at issue in *Windsor*, most married same-sex couples will not be affected because most people generally are not subject to the estate tax. In 2012, roughly 3,600 estates, representing less than 0.2% of all deaths in 2012, are subject to the estate tax.[22] Given that so few estates are subject to the estate tax, and that the estate tax is a small portion of overall federal tax revenues,[23] the federal budgetary impact of recognizing same-sex marriages for estate tax purposes is small.[24]

Income Tax

The *Windsor* decision could affect married same-sex couples' federal income taxes in a variety of ways. All taxpayers in federally recognized same-sex marriages will be required to file as married on any return filed after September 15, 2013,[25] which may affect their marginal tax rates.[26] Other tax effects of the decision may include changes in eligibility for a variety of tax credits, as well as changes in the tax treatment of certain forms of employee compensation. These changes will, in many cases, change married same-sex couples' tax liabilities, as discussed below. There are other changes not discussed which are beyond the scope of this report.

Tax Filing Status and Tax Brackets

Before *Windsor*, married same-sex couples were generally considered single for federal income tax purposes. In cases where the couple had children, one partner would claim any children as dependents and file federal income taxes using the head of household status. The other spouse would file as single.

As a result of the ruling on Section 3 of DOMA, same-sex couples who are recognized as married under the IRC will be required to file their taxes in the same manner as married opposite-sex couples—generally either jointly ("married filing jointly") or separately ("married filing separately"). However, very few married taxpayers file separately (less than 5% of married taxpayers in 2010)[27] because it generally results in higher tax liabilities than if income taxes are filed jointly.[28]

Hence, the remainder of this report will generally describe situations where married same-sex couples, as a result of the *Windsor* decision, will file their returns jointly.

For some same-sex couples, filing status changes resulting from the *Windsor* decision may result in increased or decreased income tax liabilities. Some married same-sex couples may face a "marriage penalty," having a higher tax liability when filing taxes as a married couple than their combined tax liability when filing as two single taxpayers. Other married same-sex couples may benefit from a "marriage bonus," whereby they have a lower tax liability when filing as a couple than their combined tax liability when filing individually.

Various circumstances may make it more or less likely that couples incur a marriage penalty or a marriage bonus when filing their income taxes.[29] Marriage penalties are more likely among couples where both partners earn similar incomes. Couples with a greater disparity in earnings are more likely to experience a marriage bonus. Most couples in which one spouse earns less than 5% (or none) of the family's total income will experience a marriage bonus.[30]

Marriage tax penalties and bonuses are consequences of a progressive tax system, whereby higher ranges of income are subject to higher tax rates. Tax brackets refer to the range of income subject to a particular tax rate. For example, under current law, the first $17,850 of taxable income for all married joint filers is subject to a 10% tax rate (the "10% bracket"). Taxable income above $17,850 but less than $72,500 is taxed at a 15% rate (the "15% bracket"). All tax brackets for 2013 for single and married joint filers are given in the text box on the following page.

Table 1 provides an illustrative example of how the distribution of a combined income of $200,000 between partners can result in a marriage bonus or penalty.

A couple where both partners earn $100,000, having a combined income of $200,000, would experience a marriage tax penalty of $879. A couple where one partner earns $50,000 and the other $150,000, also having a combined income of $200,000, would have a marriage tax bonus of $557.

Table 1. Example of Marriage Penalties and Bonuses Among Same-Sex Couples

Ordinary Income Split between Partners	Combined Tax Liability		Change in Tax Liability
	Unmarried Partners	Married Partners	
Partner A: $50,000 Partner B: $150,000	$38,422	$37,866	$557 (bonus)
Partner A: $100,000 Partner B: $100,000	$36,987	$37,866	-$879 (penalty)

Source: 2013 Data from the Tax Policy Center. See http://taxpolicycenter.org/taxfacts/marriagepenaltycalculator.cfm.

In the example in *Table 1*, when each taxpayer earning $100,000 was taxed as a single individual, each had earnings that put them in the lower end of the 28% tax bracket.[31] Thus, most of their income falls into the 25% bracket or below. A feature of the U.S. income tax system is that the 25% tax bracket for married filing jointly is less than twice as large as the 25% bracket for singles. Thus, when treated as a married couple, a greater proportion of the couples' combined income falls into the higher 28% tax bracket. The marriage tax penalty results from a greater proportion of the couples' combined income being taxed at the 28% rate.

The 2001 and 2003 tax cuts (which were extended permanently for most taxpayers by the American Taxpayer Relief Act of 2012 (P.L. 112-240)) reduced or eliminated marriage penalties for many middle-income taxpayers.[33] One way these laws reduced penalties was by making certain tax brackets for married joint filers twice as large as the equivalent bracket for single filers.[34] Specifically, the 2001 and 2003 tax cuts increased the size of 10% and 15% tax brackets for married taxpayers filing jointly such that brackets for married filing jointly became twice the size of single brackets.[35] Hence, if two single individuals in the 10% or 15% bracket marry, their combined income would either still be in the 15% bracket (marriage would be tax-neutral) or in the 10% bracket (a marriage bonus since a portion of their income would be taxed at a lower rate, 10% versus 15%).

As an example, take a single taxpayer with taxable income of $1,000. This taxpayer would be in the 10% bracket. Suppose this taxpayer marries an individual with taxable earnings of $10,000, putting them in the 15% bracket for individuals. With a combined income of $11,000, this couple would be in the 10% bracket when married filing jointly. With no income being taxed at the 15% rate, this couple would experience a marriage tax bonus.

Tax Brackets for Single Filers and Married Joint Filers, 2013[32]

Bracket (tax rate)	Single Taxable Income (over-but not over)	Married Filing Jointly Taxable Income (over-but not over)
10%	$0-$8,925	$0-$17,850
15%	$8,925-$36,250	$17,850-$72,500
25%	$36,250-$87,850	$72,500-$146,400
28%	$87,850-$183,250	$146,400-$223,050
33%	$183,250-$398,350	$223,050-$398,350
35%	$398,350-$400,000	$398,350-$450,000
39.6%	$400,000-	$450,000-

Dual-worker couples with income above the 15% bracket threshold could face a penalty because higher tax brackets for joint filers are less than twice as wide as those for single filers. Ultimately for those taxpayers with income above the 15% bracket ($36,250 for singles and $72,500 for joint filers in 2013), the distribution of income between both spouses and the presence or absence of children will determine whether marriage results in a penalty or bonus.

Marriage penalties may be more likely for couples with children for several reasons. Many involve tax credits, which are discussed below. However, another reason involves the changes in filing status and resulting changes in tax brackets. Prior to the *Windsor* decision, married same-sex couples with children could not file a federal tax return as a married couple. Instead, one partner would file as a head of household, claiming the children as a dependents. The other would file as single. As a result of the *Windsor* decision, couples with children whose marriage is federally recognized will be required to file as married. Although allowed to file joint returns, they may find that they will be in a higher tax bracket than they were when they filed as head of household and single. Since tax brackets above the 15% bracket for married couples filing jointly are less than the combined equivalent levels if one of the taxpayers were filing as head of household and the other as single, married same-sex couples may be subject to a marriage penalty depending on the distribution of earnings between the spouses.

Other Selected Income Tax Issues

As a result of the *Windsor* decision, other aspects of married same-sex couples' income taxes may change, including the amount of or eligibility for credits and the tax treatment of certain forms of employee compensation.

Income Tax Credits

After the *Windsor* decision, the tax liabilities of same-sex couples with children may change since marriage, as recognized for federal tax purposes, can affect the amount of certain tax credits, especially those that benefit taxpayers with children. Generally, tax credits are structured such that the amount of the credit falls when income exceeds a certain threshold, ultimately phasing out to zero. When marriage results in a combined income that is in a credit's phase-out range (or is so high the taxpayers are ineligible for the credit), the credit amount may be reduced resulting in increased tax liability. Some of the credits that are subject to income limitations are described below:

- The Earned Income Tax Credit (EITC): The value of the earned income tax credit (EITC) is reduced for many low-income dual earner couples when they are married. Marriage penalties occur when the joint income of the married couple pushes them into the EITC phase-out range or results in the couple being ineligible for the credit.[36]
- The Child and Dependent Care Credit: The amount of the child and dependent care credit is limited to no more than the income of the lower earning spouse. If one spouse has no income, the couple generally would not qualify for the credit.
- The Child Tax Credit: The value of the child tax credit phases out as a taxpayer's income rises above a certain income level.[37] The phase-out threshold for married couples is less than twice that for unmarried individuals. As a result, two unmarried individuals might each qualify for the credit but receive a smaller credit or become ineligible for it if married.
- Education Tax Credits: The income levels at which taxpayers are ineligible for education tax credits tend to be twice as high for married couples as for singles. The ultimate value of the credit as a result of marriage will depend on the distribution of income among spouses. Marriage is unlikely to affect the overall credit amount among couples whose income is equally distributed between the two partners. However, among couples whose income is less evenly distributed, the value of their education credit will depend on the income level of the

individuals who incur education expenses, and could increase or decrease as a result of marriage depending on the taxpayers' particular circumstances.

- Adoption Credit: The Windsor decision also has implications for same-sex couples claiming the adoption tax credit. The adoption credit is generally not allowed when adopting a spouse's child.38 Therefore, the Windsor decision may mean that some same-sex partners who might otherwise have been able to claim an adoption credit will no longer be able to do so.

Non-Taxable Employee Compensation

The *Windsor* decision will affect whether certain forms of employee compensation are nontaxable, including contributions to dependent care flexible spending accounts (DCFSA) and the employer contributions for employer-provided health insurance plans.

Under current law, taxpayers with children may contribute up to $5,000 to a DCFSA. The total amount of contributions that are tax exempt for any tax return is $5,000 without regard to the number of children or the number of parents. Hence, a married couple can put a maximum of $5,000 in a DCFSA, the same maximum amount an individual can put in these accounts. Therefore, any amount in excess of $5,000 would be included in taxable income for the married couple. Same-sex married couples who each have contributed to a DCFSA may find that part of their account becomes taxable even though their individual incomes make them eligible for the child and dependent care credit. If each partner had a child and each was contributing to a DCFSA, they may have over-contributed in the first year in which they file as a married couple. In subsequent years, they would be limited to putting $5,000 in the DCFSA, though they could divide that amount between themselves.[39]

In contrast to the effect on DCFSA, the *Windsor* decision will provide tax benefits to married same-sex couples who are covered by an employer-sponsored health insurance plan. When an employee elects to purchase employer-provided health insurance, the employer generally pays for part of the premium. The employer's contribution to an individual or family plan generally is not considered taxable income to the employee. However, before the *Windsor* decision, same-sex employees who purchased an employer-sponsored family health plan were taxed on the estimated value of the employer's contribution toward the premiums for the same-sex spouse. Opposite-sex couples are not taxed on the portion of health insurance premiums the employer pays for the opposite-sex spouse. After *Windsor*, the estimated value of the employer's contribution to health-insurance coverage for an employee's same-sex spouse will be nontaxable, reducing tax liability.

Potential Income Tax Consequences of the Windsor Decision

Research quantifying the income tax consequences of marriage for opposite-sex couples may be useful for understanding the potential tax consequences of marriage for same-sex couples. Applying the 2007 tax code to cohabiting couples, Lin and Tong (2012) found that roughly half of couples who marry would have a marriage tax penalty.[40] Most of the remaining couples (38%) were estimated to have marriage tax bonuses. On average, marriage resulted in an increase in tax liability of $450 per couple. However, since certain research indicates that the demographic characteristics of opposite-sex couples differ from those of same-sex couples (e.g., within-couple distribution of earnings, number of children), marriage tax consequences amongst the population of same-sex couples may not follow the same patterns as found for opposite-sex couples.[41]

As discussed earlier in this report, if same-sex couples tend to have two income earners with similar incomes, these couples are likely to face marriage tax penalties, especially if their combined income were to push them above the 15% tax bracket. On the other hand, same-sex couples who marry are less likely to have children than opposite-sex couples which would lead to more marriage tax bonuses, particularly for lower-income couples.[42] On balance, as indicated by the estimates that suggest same-sex marriage will result in additional federal revenues,[43] the value of marriage tax penalties is expected to exceed the total value of marriage tax bonuses for same-sex couples.[44] Reportedly, the Treasury has noted that data on the proportion of married same-sex couples who would face marriage tax penalties or bonuses is lacking.[45]

Recognizing same-sex marriages for federal income tax purposes would likely result in additional federal income tax revenues, although available estimates suggest the budgetary impact would be small. In 2004, the Congressional Budget Office (CBO) estimated that recognition of same-sex marriages would increase federal income tax revenues by $200 million to $400 million per year between 2005 and 2010.[46] Others contend that the revenue gains would be smaller than CBO's estimates, somewhere in the $20 million to $40 million range annually.[47] Relative to the magnitude of total individual income tax revenues—$1.1 trillion in 2012—the revenues that might be raised by recognizing same-sex marriages for federal tax purposes represent less than one-tenth of one percent of income tax revenues.[48]

AMENDING TAX RETURNS

Before *Windsor*, all same-sex married couples were required to file their federal income tax returns as unmarried individuals. The August 29, 2013, Treasury and IRS ruling made clear that taxpayers who were in same-sex marriages for one or more open prior tax years may file amended returns to change their filing status to that of a married couple. For most taxpayers, this means that amended returns can be filed for tax years 2010, 2011, and 2012.[49] Filing amended returns is an option, but not a requirement. Thus, taxpayers may choose to file an amended return if doing so will result in a refund. Taxpayers may choose to file amended returns to exclude from income certain fringe benefits, such as health insurance coverage, provided to a same-sex spouse.[50] Taxpayers in legal same-sex marriages who want to amend prior year's tax returns for reasons other than changing their filing status should proceed with caution since it is unclear whether they would be required to change their filing status if amending the return after September 16, 2013.[51] If such a change were required, it might negate any benefit they would otherwise derive from amending the return depending upon the facts and circumstances involved in their (and their spouses') returns.

The unlimited marital deduction under the estate tax was at issue in *Windsor*. The Court determined that the estate was allowed to transfer all assets to Ms. Windsor, the surviving spouse, without incurring estate taxes. Surviving spouses of same-sex marriages may choose to file an amended estate tax return for open years if the decedent's estate was subject to estate taxes as a result of not using the unlimited marital deduction.

End Notes

[1] United States v. Windsor, 570 U.S. ____; 133 S. Ct. 2675 (2013). No. 12-307, slip op. available at http://www.supremecourt.gov/opinions/12pdf/12-307_6j37.pdf.

[2] Although the estate tax was the motivating issue in the Windsor decision, as discussed later in this report, few married same-sex couples will be affected by changes in the administration of the estate tax.

[3] 1 U.S.C. § 7.

[4] P.L. 104-199.

[5] According to Section 3 of the Defense of Marriage Act (DOMA), "In determining the meaning of any Act of Congress, or of any ruling, regulation, or interpretation of the various administrative bureaus and agencies of the United States, the word 'marriage' means only a legal union between one man and one woman as husband and wife, and the

word 'spouse' refers only to a person of the opposite-sex who is a husband or a wife." 1 U.S.C. §7.

[6] U.S. General Accounting Office, Defense of Marriage Act: Update to Prior Report, GAO-04-353R, January 23, 2004.

[7] Using tables provided by GAO, CRS found that in 2004, there were 198 sections of the Internal Revenue Code (IRC) in which marital status was a factor. See Appendix 1 and Appendix 2 in GAO-04-353R and Enclosure II in U.S. General Accounting Office, Defense of Marriage Act, OGC-97-16, January 31, 1997.

[8] See Rev. Rul 2013-17. Available at http://www.irs.gov/pub/irs-drop/rr-13-17.pdf. There is a possibility that some provisions in the U.S. Code or the respective regulations implementing them may need modification of wording so that they can apply to married same-sex couples.

[9] Similarly, guidance from the Office of Personnel Management indicates that, for purposes of eligibility for specific federal employee benefits, legal same-sex marriages will be recognized "regardless of an employee's or annuitant's state of residency." OPM, Benefits Administration Letter, No. 13-203 (Jul. 17, 2013). Available at http://www.opm.gov/retirement-services/publications-forms/benefits-administration-letters/2013/13-203.pdf. As of June 2013, 13 states (California, Connecticut, Delaware, Iowa, Maine, Maryland, Massachusetts, Minnesota, New Hampshire, New York, Rhode Island, Vermont, and Washington), and the District of Columbia recognized same-sex marriages. Additionally, some counties in New Mexico and one in Pennsylvania have been issuing marriage licenses to same sex couples. Some of the counties in New Mexico are doing so pursuant to court order, while in at least one other county, the county clerk began issuing marriage licenses without court order. Associated Press, "New Mexico judge upholds county same-sex marriage ruling, orders issuing of licenses," Washington Post, September 4, 2013. Available at http://www.washingtonpost.com/national/new-mexico-judge-upholds-county-same-sex-marriage-ruling-ordersissuing-of-licenses/2013/09/04/bc6dc7a2-158a-11e3-961c-f22d3aaf19ab_story.html. In Pennsylvania, the Montgomery County clerk began issuing the licenses despite state law to the contrary. The Pennsylvania Health Department filed a case against the clerk. The judge hearing the case has indicated that he will rule quickly. Miranda Leitsinger, Pa. judge hears arguments in landmark gay marriage case, Sept. 4, 2013, NBC News. Available at http://usnews.nbcnews.com/ _news/2013/09/04/20311916-pa-judge-hears-arguments-in-landmark-gay-marriage-case?lite&preview=true.

[10] This ruling clarifies previous uncertainty, where it was unclear if recognition of same-sex marriage for federal tax purposes would depend on recognition of same-sex marriage in a couple's state of residence. The Court in the Windsor decision wrote, "The federal statute is invalid, for no legitimate purpose overcomes the purpose and effect to disparage and to injure those whom the State, by its marriage laws, sought to protect in personhood and dignity. By seeking to displace this protection and treating those people as living in marriages less respected than others, the federal law is in violation of the Fifth Amendment. This opinion and its holding are confined to those lawful marriages." U.S. v. Windsor, 570 U.S. ____ ; 133 S.Ct. at 2696. No. 12-307, slip op. at 25-26 available at http://www.supremecourt.gov/ opinions/12pdf/12-307_6j37.pdf.

[11] It is important to note that a civil union is a legal protection conferred at the state, not the federal, level. As such a variety of benefits discussed in this report may not apply to civil unions.

[12] This calculation is based on the 2011 American Community Survey (ACS)—the most recent data available—which asks respondents their sex as well as the sex of their partner. The respondent can identify a potential partner as a husband, wife, or an unmarried partner—although the question does not require the respondent to specify whether the partner is legally recognized as a spouse. For more information, see American Community Survey, http://www.census.gov/acs/www/about_the_survey/forms_ and_ instructions/. For ACS data see http://www.census.gov/ hhes/samesex/data/acs.html.

[13] See Lydia Beyoud, "Legal Same-Sex Marriage Recognized for Federal Tax Purposes, IRS, Treasury Says," Bloomberg BNA Daily Tax Report, Aug. 30, 2013.

[14] Lydia Beyoud, "Domestic Partners: Practitioners Say Major Guidance Needed from Federal Agencies for Same-Sex Couples," BNA Daily Tax Report, July 1, 2013.

[15] From the ACS, supra footnote 12. These data are reported as the percentage of same-sex households where the partners are reported as spouses. It does not necessarily reflect those spouses who are legally married. For ACS data see http://www.census.gov/ hhes/samesex/data/acs.html.

[16] Partners in same-sex couples may consider themselves "spouses" even if they are not legally married if, for example, they are in a civil union or a domestic partnership. Hence these statistics should not be interpreted as the number of same-sex couples who are legally married.

[17] When Edith Windsor's wife died, her wife's estate was obligated to pay approximately $363,000 in federal estate taxes. Had Edith Windsor been married to a man, she would have qualified for the spousal exemption and the estate would not have been taxed at the time of her spouse's death.

[18] For an overview of the estate tax, see CRS Report R42959, The Estate and Gift Tax Provisions of the American Taxpayer Relief Act of 2012, by Jane G. Gravelle.

[19] Recognition of same-sex marriages for the purposes of the federal estate tax can only result in a reduction in estate taxes: "marriage tax bonuses."

[20] This exemption amount is adjusted annually for inflation.

[21] An estate tax return must be timely filed to affect this transfer even if the estate would not otherwise be required to file a return.

[22] See Tax Policy Center analysis of 2013 Budget Proposals, available at http://www. taxpolicycenter.org/taxtopics/ 2013-Restore-the-Estate-Gift-and-Generation-Skipping-Transfer-Tax.cfm.

[23] In 2012, 1.2% of total federal revenue was collected through the estate tax.

[24] This was the conclusion reached in a 2004 Congressional Budget Office (CBO) report. CBO also noted that same-sex spouses may be more likely than opposite-sex spouses to make charitable bequests from their estates, although no specific evidence was given in support of this claim. See Congressional Budget Office, The Potential Budgetary Impact of Recognizing Same-Sex Marriages, Washington, DC, June 21, 2004, http://www.cbo. gov/publication/15740.

[25] September 16, 2013, is the effective date of Rev. Rul. 2013-17.

[26] 26 U.S.C. §§1(a), (d); 6013; 7703.

[27] In 2010, 56.1 million married taxpayers filed income tax returns, of which 2.5 million were filed as married filing separately. See the IRS Statistics of Information (SOI), Table 1.2, http://www.irs.gov/uac/SOI-Tax-Stats—IndividualStatistical-Tables-by-Size-of-Adjusted-Gross-Income.

[28] Filing separately tends to be least advantageous to married couples, since they are denied a variety of tax benefits or receive smaller benefits. See Leslie A. Whittington and Updated

by James Alm, "Marriage Penalty," in The Encyclopedia of Taxation and Tax Policy, ed. Joseph J. Cordes, Robert D. Ebel and Jane G. Gravelle, 2nd ed. (Washington, D.C.: The Urban Institute Press, 2005), p. 252.

[29] For evidence on the tax consequences of marriage for cohabiting couples, see Emily Y. Lin and Patricia K. Tong, "Marriage and Taxes: What Can We Learn from Tax Returns Filed by Cohabiting Couples?" National Tax Journal, vol. 65, no. 4 (December 2012), pp. 807-826.

[30] Ibid., p. 818. Using 2007 data, it was found that only 3% of cohabiting couples where one spouse earned less than 5% of combined income prior to marriage experienced a marriage tax penalty, 21% saw no change in tax liability, and 77% had a marriage bonus.

[31] For 2013 statutory marginal tax rates and tax brackets, see CRS Report RL32808, Overview of the Federal Tax System, by Molly F. Sherlock and Donald J. Marples.

[32] See IRS Revenue Procedure 2013-15, http://www.irs.gov/pub/irs-drop/rp-13-15.pdf.

[33] For more information on all the provisions of the Bush-era tax cuts, including marriage penalty relief, see Table 1 in CRS Report R42894, An Overview of the Tax Provisions in the American Taxpayer Relief Act of 2012 , by Margot L. Crandall-Hollick.

[34] A tax bracket is a range of income that is subject to a specific tax rate. (For example, if hypothetically income between $10,000 and $20,000 was subject to a 7% tax rate, that range of income would be called the 7% tax bracket.)

[35] The 2001 and 2003 tax cuts made the standard deduction for married couples twice as large as the standard deduction for individuals and coordinated phase-out thresholds for certain tax benefits. These provisions were made permanent by P.L. 112-240.

[36] In 2013, a childless taxpayer can receive a maximum credit of $487, while the maximum values of the credit for taxpayers with children are $3,250 for a taxpayer with one child, $5,372 for a taxpayer with two children, and $6,044 for a taxpayer with three or more children. These levels are adjusted annually for inflation. For more information, see CRS Report RL31768, The Earned Income Tax Credit (EITC): An Overview, by Christine Scott. It is possible that low-income couples with children could have a marriage tax bonus if they were in the phase-in range for the EITC.

[37] Currently, the phase-out threshold is $110,000 for couples filing jointly and $75,000 for unmarried individuals.

[38] For general background on the adoption tax credit, see CRS Report RL33633, Tax Benefits for Families: Adoption, by Christine Scott.

[39] Filing separate returns would be the least beneficial because no child care expenses are recognized for married people who file separately.

[40] Emily Y. Lin and Patricia K. Tong, "Marriage and Taxes: What Can We Learn from Tax Returns Filed by Cohabiting Couples?" National Tax Journal, vol. 65, no. 4 (December 2012), pp. 807-826.

[41] Differences in demographic characteristics between same-sex and opposite-sex couples are noted in Adam Stevenson, "The Labor Supply and Tax Revenue Consequences of Federal Same-Sex Marriage Legalization," National Tax Journal, vol. 65, no. 4 (December 2012), pp. 783-806.

[42] Stevenson, supra note 40.

[43] Congressional Budget Office, The Potential Budgetary Impact of Recognizing Same-Sex Marriages, Washington, DC, June 21, 2004, http://www.cbo.gov/publication/15740 and Stevenson, supra note 40.

[44] Over time, as a result of the Windsor decision regarding same-sex marriage, the social and economic characteristics of same-sex couples who legally marry may change. For

example, more married same-sex couples may choose to have or adopt children. Or one spouse may choose to leave the workforce. Such changes could have an impact on the federal income tax liability of the couple.

[45] Beyoud, supra footnote 13.

[46] Congressional Budget Office, The Potential Budgetary Impact of Recognizing Same-Sex Marriages, Washington, DC, June 21, 2004, http://www.cbo.gov/publication/15740.

[47] Stevenson, supra note 40.

[48] Others have also noted that while recognizing same-sex marriages for federal tax purposes will likely result in additional federal revenues, the effect is expected to be small. See Diana Furchtgott-Roth, "Same-Sex Marriage Decisions Won't Affect Uncle Sam's Bottom Line," Tax Notes, July 1, 2013, pp. 75-77.

[49] Generally, taxpayers may file amended returns within the three years after the filing date of the return or two years after the tax was paid, whichever is later. These are considered "open years." However, there may be other considerations in determining whether to amend a prior year's return. One might be whether one wants to extend the time in which the return can be examined.

[50] Where health insurance for a same-sex spouse was included in income, the taxpayer may be able to recover excess Social Security and Medicare paid based on the income recognized for the same-sex insurance coverage. Employers will be able to file Form 941-X to claim refunds or adjustments for overpayment of both the employer's and employee's portions of Social Security and Medicare tax. The IRS is expected to provide guidance soon regarding procedures to be followed. Answers to Frequently Asked Questions for Individuals of the Same Sex Who Are Married Under State Law, Q. 12, Internal Revenue Service. Available at http://www.irs.gov/uac/Answers-to-Frequently-AskedQuestions-for-Same-Sex-Married-Couples.

[51] IRS guidance addresses the effect of Windsor on original returns filed after September 15, 2013, as well as the option for amending to change the filing status on a return to MFJ or MFS, but does not address whether an amended return filed after September 15, 2013 must be filed using a married filing status. Id. Q. 2.

In: Same-Sex Marriage Bans ... ISBN: 978-1-63463-844-9
Editor: Maxine Dunn

Chapter 3

DECISION OF THE SUPREME COURT OF THE UNITED STATES IN THE CASE OF UNITED STATES V. WINDSOR, EXECUTOR OF THE ESTATE OF SPYER, ET AL.*

(Slip Opinion) OCTOBER TERM, 2012

Syllabus

NOTE: Where it is feasible, a syllabus (headnote) will be released, as is being done in connection with this case, at the time the opinion is issued. The syllabus constitutes no part of the opinion of the Court but has been prepared by the Reporter of Decisions for the convenience of the reader. See *United States* v. *Detroit Timber & Lumber Co.,* 200 U. S. 321, 337.

* This is an edited, reformatted and augmented version of the official slip opinion as delivered by the U.S. Supreme Court on June 26, 2013.

SUPREME COURT OF THE UNITED STATES

Syllabus

UNITED STATES *v.* WINDSOR, EXECUTOR OF THE ESTATE OF SPYER, ET AL.

CERTIORARI TO THE UNITED STATES COURT OF APPEALS FOR THE SECOND CIRCUIT

No. 12–307. Argued March 27, 2013—Decided June 26, 2013

The State of New York recognizes the marriage of New York residents Edith Windsor and Thea Spyer, who wed in Ontario, Canada, in 2007. When Spyer died in 2009, she left her entire estate to Windsor. Windsor sought to claim the federal estate tax exemption for surviving spouses, but was barred from doing so by §3 of the federal Defense of Marriage Act (DOMA), which amended the Dictionary Act—a law providing rules of construction for over 1,000 federal laws and the whole realm of federal regulations—to define "marriage" and "spouse" as excluding same-sex partners. Windsor paid $363,053 in estate taxes and sought a refund, which the Internal Revenue Service denied. Windsor brought this refund suit, contending that DOMA violates the principles of equal protection incorporated in the Fifth Amendment. While the suit was pending, the Attorney General notified the Speaker of the House of Representatives that the Department of Justice would no longer defend §3's constitutionality. In response, the Bipartisan Legal Advisory Group (BLAG) of the House of Representatives voted to intervene in the litigation to defend §3's constitutionality. The District Court permitted the intervention. On the merits, the court ruled against the United States, finding §3 unconstitutional and ordering the Treasury to refund Windsor's tax with interest. The Second Circuit affirmed. The United States has not complied with the judgment.

***Held*:**

1. This Court has jurisdiction to consider the merits of the case. This case clearly presented a concrete disagreement between opposing parties that was suitable for judicial resolution in the District Court, but the Executive's decision not to defend §3's constitutionality in court while continuing to deny refunds and assess deficiencies introduces a complication. Given the Government's concession, *amicus* contends, once the District Court ordered

the refund, the case should have ended and the appeal been dismissed. But this argument elides the distinction between Article III's jurisdictional requirements and the prudential limits on its exercise, which are "essentially matters of judicial self-governance." *Warth* v. *Seldin*, 422 U. S. 490, 500. Here, the United States retains a stake sufficient to support Article III jurisdiction on appeal and in this Court. The refund it was ordered to pay Windsor is "a real and immediate economic injury," *Hein* v. *Freedom From Religion Foundation, Inc.*, 551 U. S. 587, 599, even if the Executive disagrees with §3 of DOMA. Windsor's ongoing claim for funds that the United States refuses to pay thus establishes a controversy sufficient for Article III jurisdiction. Cf. *INS* v. *Chadha*, 462 U. S. 919.

Prudential considerations, however, demand that there be "concrete adverseness which sharpens the presentation of issues upon which the court so largely depends for illumination of difficult constitutional questions." *Baker* v. *Carr*, 369 U. S. 186, 204. Unlike Article III requirements—which must be satisfied by the parties before judicial consideration is appropriate—prudential factors that counsel against hearing this case are subject to "countervailing considerations [that] may outweigh the concerns underlying the usual reluctance to exert judicial power." *Warth, supra,* at 500–501. One such consideration is the extent to which adversarial presentation of the issues is ensured by the participation of *amici curiae* prepared to defend with vigor the legislative act's constitutionality. See *Chadha, supra,* at 940. Here, BLAG's substantial adversarial argument for §3's constitutionality satisfies prudential concerns that otherwise might counsel against hearing an appeal from a decision with which the principal parties agree. This conclusion does not mean that it is appropriate for the Executive as a routine exercise to challenge statutes in court instead of making the case to Congress for amendment or repeal. But this case is not routine, and BLAG's capable defense ensures that the prudential issues do not cloud the merits question, which is of immediate importance to the Federal Government and to hundreds of thousands of persons. Pp. 5–13.

2. DOMA is unconstitutional as a deprivation of the equal liberty of persons that is protected by the Fifth Amendment. Pp. 13–26.

(a) By history and tradition the definition and regulation of marriage has been treated as being within the authority and realm of the separate States. Congress has enacted discrete statutes to regulate the meaning of marriage in order to further federal policy, but DOMA, with a directive applicable to over 1,000 federal statutes and the whole realm of federal regulations, has a far greater reach.

Its operation is also directed to a class of persons that the laws of New York, and of 11 other States, have sought to protect. Assessing the validity of that intervention requires discussing the historical and traditional extent of state power and authority over marriage.

Subject to certain constitutional guarantees, see, *e.g., Loving* v. *Virginia*, 388 U. S. 1, "regulation of domestic relations" is "an area that has long been regarded as a virtually exclusive province of the States," *Sosna* v. *Iowa*, 419 U. S. 393, 404.

The significance of state responsibilities for the definition and regulation of marriage dates to the Nation's beginning; for "when the Constitution was adopted the common understanding was that the domestic relations of husband and wife and parent and child were matters reserved to the States," *Ohio ex rel. Popovici* v. *Agler*, 280 U. S. 379, 383–384. Marriage laws may vary from State to State, but they are consistent within each State.

DOMA rejects this long-established precept. The State's decision to give this class of persons the right to marry conferred upon them a dignity and status of immense import. But the Federal Government uses the state-defined class for the opposite purpose—to impose restrictions and disabilities. The question is whether the resulting injury and indignity is a deprivation of an essential part of the liberty protected by the Fifth Amendment, since what New York treats as alike the federal law deems unlike by a law designed to injure the same class the State seeks to protect. New York's actions were a proper exercise of its sovereign authority. They reflect both the community's considered perspective on the historical roots of the institution of marriage and its evolving understanding of the meaning of equality. Pp. 13–20.

(b) By seeking to injure the very class New York seeks to protect, DOMA violates basic due process and equal protection principles applicable to the Federal Government. The Constitution's guarantee of equality "must at the very least mean that a bare congressional desire to harm a politically unpopular group cannot" justify disparate treatment of that group. *Department of Agriculture* v. *Moreno*, 413 U. S. 528, 534–535. DOMA cannot survive under these principles. Its unusual deviation from the tradition of recognizing and accepting state definitions of marriage operates to deprive same-sex couples of the benefits and responsibilities that come with federal recognition of their marriages.

This is strong evidence of a law having the purpose and effect of disapproval of a class recognized and protected by state law. DOMA's avowed purpose and practical effect are to impose a disadvantage, a separate status, and so a stigma upon all who enter into same-sex marriages made lawful by the unquestioned authority of the States.

DOMA's history of enactment and its own text demonstrate that interference with the equal dignity of same-sex marriages, conferred by the States in the exercise of their sovereign power, was more than an incidental effect of the federal statute. It was its essence. BLAG's arguments are just as candid about the congressional purpose. DOMA's operation in practice confirms this purpose. It frustrates New York's objective of eliminating inequality by writing inequality into the entire United States Code.

DOMA's principal effect is to identify and make unequal a subset of state-sanctioned marriages. It contrives to deprive some couples married under the laws of their State, but not others, of both rights and responsibilities, creating two contradictory marriage regimes within the same State. It also forces same-sex couples to live as married for the purpose of state law but unmarried for the purpose of federal law, thus diminishing the stability and predictability of basic personal relations the State has found it proper to acknowledge and protect. Pp. 20–26.

699 F. 3d 169, affirmed.

KENNEDY, J., delivered the opinion of the Court, in which GINSBURG, BREYER, SOTOMAYOR, and KAGAN, JJ., joined. ROBERTS, C. J., filed a dissenting opinion. SCALIA, J., filed a dissenting opinion, in which THOMAS, J., joined, and in which ROBERTS, C. J., joined as to Part I. ALITO, J., filed a dissenting opinion, in which THOMAS, J., joined as to Parts II and III.

Opinion of the Court

NOTICE: This opinion is subject to formal revision before publication in the preliminary print of the United States Reports. Readers are requested to notify the Reporter of Decisions, Supreme Court of the United States, Washington, D. C. 20543, of any typographical or other formal errors, in order that corrections may be made before the preliminary print goes to press.

Supreme Court of the United States

No. 12–307

UNITED STATES, PETITIONER *v.* EDITH SCHLAIN WINDSOR, IN HER CAPACITY AS EXECUTOR OF THE ESTATE OF THEA CLARA SPYER, ET AL.

ON WRIT OF CERTIORARI TO THE UNITED STATES COURT OF APPEALS FOR THE SECOND CIRCUIT

[June 26, 2013]

JUSTICE KENNEDY delivered the opinion of the Court.

Two women then resident in New York were married in a lawful ceremony in Ontario, Canada, in 2007. Edith Windsor and Thea Spyer returned to their home in New York City. When Spyer died in 2009, she left her entire estate to Windsor. Windsor sought to claim the estate tax exemption for surviving spouses. She was barred from doing so, however, by a federal law, the Defense of Marriage Act, which excludes a same-sex partner from the definition of "spouse" as that term is used in federal statutes. Windsor paid the taxes but filed suit to challenge the constitutionality of this provision. The United States District Court and the Court of Appeals ruled that this portion of the statute is unconstitutional and ordered the United States to pay Windsor a refund. This Court granted certiorari and now affirms the judgment in Windsor's favor.

I

In 1996, as some States were beginning to consider the concept of same-sex marriage, see, *e.g.*, *Baehr* v. *Lewin*, 74 Haw. 530, 852 P. 2d 44 (1993), and before any State had acted to permit it, Congress enacted the Defense of Marriage Act (DOMA), 110 Stat. 2419. DOMA contains two operative sections: Section 2, which has not been challenged here, allows States to refuse to recognize same-sex marriages performed under the laws of other States. See 28 U. S. C. §1738C.

Section 3 is at issue here. It amends the Dictionary Act in Title 1, §7, of the United States Code to provide a federal definition of "marriage" and "spouse." Section 3 of DOMA provides as follows:

> "In determining the meaning of any Act of Congress, or of any ruling, regulation, or interpretation of the various administrative bureaus and agencies of the United States, the word 'marriage' means only a legal union between one man and one woman as husband and wife, and the word 'spouse' refers only to a person of the opposite sex who is a husband or a wife." 1 U. S. C. §7.

The definitional provision does not by its terms forbid States from enacting laws permitting same-sex marriages or civil unions or providing state benefits to residents in that status. The enactment's comprehensive definition of marriage for purposes of all federal statutes and other regulations or directives covered by its terms, however, does control over 1,000 federal laws in which marital or spousal status is addressed as a matter of federal law. See GAO, D. Shah, Defense of Marriage Act: Update to Prior Report 1 (GAO–04–353R, 2004).

Edith Windsor and Thea Spyer met in New York City in 1963 and began a long-term relationship. Windsor and Spyer registered as domestic partners when New York City gave that right to same-sex couples in 1993. Concerned about Spyer's health, the couple made the 2007 trip to Canada for their marriage, but they continued to reside in New York City. The State of New York deems their Ontario marriage to be a valid one. See 699 F. 3d 169, 177–178 (CA2 2012).

Spyer died in February 2009, and left her entire estate to Windsor. Because DOMA denies federal recognition to same-sex spouses, Windsor did not qualify for the marital exemption from the federal estate tax, which excludes from taxation "any interest in property which passes or has passed from the decedent to his surviving spouse." 26 U. S. C. §2056(a). Windsor paid $363,053 in estate taxes and sought a refund. The Internal Revenue Service denied the refund, concluding that, under DOMA, Windsor was not a "surviving spouse." Windsor commenced this refund suit in the United States District Court for the Southern District of New York. She contended that DOMA violates the guarantee of equal protection, as applied to the Federal Government through the Fifth Amendment.

While the tax refund suit was pending, the Attorney General of the United States notified the Speaker of the House of Representatives, pursuant to 28 U. S. C. §530D, that the Department of Justice would no longer defend the constitutionality of DOMA's §3. Noting that "the Department has previously defended DOMA against . . . challenges involving legally married same-sex couples," App. 184, the Attorney General informed Congress that "the

President has concluded that given a number of factors, including a documented history of discrimination, classifications based on sexual orientation should be subject to a heightened standard of scrutiny." *Id.,* at 191. The Department of Justice has submitted many §530D letters over the years refusing to defend laws it deems unconstitutional, when, for instance, a federal court has rejected the Government's defense of a statute and has issued a judgment against it. This case is unusual, however, because the §530D letter was not preceded by an adverse judgment. The letter instead reflected the Executive's own conclusion, relying on a definition still being debated and considered in the courts, that heightened equal protection scrutiny should apply to laws that classify on the basis of sexual orientation.

Although "the President . . . instructed the Department not to defend the statute in *Windsor*," he also decided "that Section 3 will continue to be enforced by the Executive Branch" and that the United States had an "interest in providing Congress a full and fair opportunity to participate in the litigation of those cases." *Id.,* at 191–193. The stated rationale for this dual-track procedure (determination of unconstitutionality coupled with ongoing enforcement) was to "recogniz[e] the judiciary as the final arbiter of the constitutional claims raised." *Id.,* at 192.

In response to the notice from the Attorney General, the Bipartisan Legal Advisory Group (BLAG) of the House of Representatives voted to intervene in the litigation to defend the constitutionality of §3 of DOMA. The Department of Justice did not oppose limited intervention by BLAG. The District Court denied BLAG's motion to enter the suit as of right, on the rationale that the United States already was represented by the Department of Justice. The District Court, however, did grant intervention by BLAG as an interested party. See Fed. Rule Civ. Proc. 24(a)(2).

On the merits of the tax refund suit, the District Court ruled against the United States. It held that §3 of DOMA is unconstitutional and ordered the Treasury to refund the tax with interest. Both the Justice Department and BLAG filed notices of appeal, and the Solicitor General filed a petition for certiorari before judgment. Before this Court acted on the petition, the Court of Appeals for the Second Circuit affirmed the District Court's judgment. It applied heightened scrutiny to classifications based on sexual orientation, as both the Department and Windsor had urged. The United States has not complied with the judgment. Windsor has not received her refund, and the Executive Branch continues to enforce §3 of DOMA.

In granting certiorari on the question of the constitutionality of §3 of DOMA, the Court requested argument on two additional questions: whether the United States' agreement with Windsor's legal position precludes further review and whether BLAG has standing to appeal the case. All parties agree that the Court has jurisdiction to decide this case; and, with the case in that framework, the Court appointed Professor Vicki Jackson as *amicus curiae* to argue the position that the Court lacks jurisdiction to hear the dispute. 568 U. S. ___ (2012). She has ably discharged her duties.

In an unrelated case, the United States Court of Appeals for the First Circuit has also held §3 of DOMA to be unconstitutional. A petition for certiorari has been filed in that case. Pet. for Cert. in *Bipartisan Legal Advisory Group* v. *Gill*, O. T. 2012, No. 12–13.

II

It is appropriate to begin by addressing whether either the Government or BLAG, or both of them, were entitled to appeal to the Court of Appeals and later to seek certiorari and appear as parties here.

There is no dispute that when this case was in the District Court it presented a concrete disagreement between opposing parties, a dispute suitable for judicial resolution. "[A] taxpayer has standing to challenge the collection of a specific tax assessment as unconstitutional; being forced to pay such a tax causes a real and immediate economic injury to the individual taxpayer." *Hein* v. *Freedom From Religion Foundation, Inc.*, 551 U. S. 587, 599 (2007) (plurality opinion) (emphasis deleted). Windsor suffered a redressable injury when she was required to pay estate taxes from which, in her view, she was exempt but for the alleged invalidity of §3 of DOMA.

The decision of the Executive not to defend the constitutionality of §3 in court while continuing to deny refunds and to assess deficiencies does introduce a complication. Even though the Executive's current position was announced before the District Court entered its judgment, the Government's agreement with Windsor's position would not have deprived the District Court of jurisdiction to entertain and resolve the refund suit; for her injury (failure to obtain a refund allegedly required by law) was concrete, persisting, and unredressed. The Government's position—agreeing with Windsor's legal contention but refusing to give it effect—meant that there was a justiciable controversy between the parties, despite what the claimant would find to be an inconsistency in that stance. Windsor, the Government, BLAG, and the *amicus* appear to agree upon that point. The disagreement is over the standing of the parties, or aspiring parties, to take an appeal in the Court of Appeals and to appear as parties in further proceedings in this Court.

The *amicus'* position is that, given the Government's concession that §3 is unconstitutional, once the District Court ordered the refund the case should have ended; and the *amicus* argues the Court of Appeals should have dismissed the appeal. The *amicus* submits that once the President agreed with Windsor's legal position and the District Court issued its judgment, the parties were no longer adverse. From this standpoint the United States was a prevailing party below, just as Windsor was. Accordingly, the *amicus* reasons, it is inappropriate for this Court to grant certiorari and proceed to rule on the merits; for the United States seeks no redress from the judgment entered against it.

This position, however, elides the distinction between two principles: the jurisdictional requirements of Article III and the prudential limits on its exercise. See *Warth* v. *Seldin*, 422 U. S. 490, 498 (1975). The latter are "essentially matters of judicial self-governance." *Id.*, at 500. The Court has kept these two strands separate: "Article III standing, which enforces the Constitution's case-orcontroversy requirement, see *Lujan* v. *Defenders of Wildlife,* 504 U. S. 555, 559–562 (1992); and prudential standing, which embodies 'judicially self-imposed limits on the exer- cise of federal jurisdiction,' *Allen* [v. *Wright*,] 468 U. S. [737,] 751 [(1984)]." *Elk Grove Unified School Dist.* v. *Newdow*, 542 U. S. 1, 11–12 (2004).

The requirements of Article III standing are familiar:

> "First, the plaintiff must have suffered an 'injury in fact'—an invasion of a legally protected interest which is (a) concrete and particularized, and (b) 'actual or imminent, not "conjectural or hypothetical."' Second, there must be a causal connection between the injury and the conduct complained of—the injury has to be 'fairly . . . trace[able] to the challenged action of the defendant, and not . . . th[e] result [of] the independent action of some third party not before the court.' Third, it must be 'likely,' as opposed to merely 'speculative,' that the injury will be 'redressed by a favor- able decision.'" *Lujan, supra,* at 560–561 (footnote and citations omitted).

Rules of prudential standing, by contrast, are more flex- ible "rule[s] . . . of federal appellate practice," *Deposit Guaranty Nat. Bank* v. *Roper*, 445 U. S. 326, 333 (1980), designed to protect the courts from "decid[ing] abstract questions of wide public significance even [when] other governmental institutions may be more competent to ad- dress the questions and even though judicial intervention may be unnecessary to protect individual rights." *Warth, supra,* at 500.

In this case the United States retains a stake sufficient to support Article III jurisdiction on appeal and in proceedings before this Court. The judgment in question orders the United States to pay Windsor the refund she seeks. An order directing the Treasury to pay money is "a real and immediate economic injury," *Hein*, 551 U. S., at 599, indeed as real and immediate as an order directing an individual to pay a tax. That the Executive may welcome this order to pay the refund if it is accompanied by the constitutional ruling it wants does not eliminate the injury to the national Treasury if payment is made, or to the taxpayer if it is not. The judgment orders the United States to pay money that it would not disburse but for the court's order. The Government of the United States has a valid legal argument that it is injured even if the Executive disagrees with §3 of DOMA, which results in Windsor's liability for the tax. Windsor's ongoing claim for funds that the United States refuses to pay thus establishes a controversy sufficient for Article III jurisdiction. It would be a different case if the Executive had taken the further step of paying Windsor the refund to which she was entitled under the District Court's ruling.

This Court confronted a comparable case in *INS* v. *Chadha*, 462 U. S. 919 (1983). A statute by its terms allowed one House of Congress to order the Immigration and Naturalization Service (INS) to deport the respondent Chadha. There, as here, the Executive determined that the statute was unconstitutional, and "the INS presented the Executive's views on the constitutionality of the House action to the Court of Appeals." *Id.,* at 930. The INS, however, continued to abide by the statute, and "the INS brief to the Court of Appeals did not alter the agency's decision to comply with the House action ordering deportation of Chadha." *Ibid.* This Court held "that the INS was sufficiently aggrieved by the Court of Appeals decision prohibiting it from taking action it would otherwise take," *ibid.,* regardless of whether the agency welcomed the judgment. The necessity of a "case or controversy" to satisfy Article III was defined as a requirement that the Court's "'decision will have real meaning: if we rule for Chadha, he will not be deported; if we uphold [the statute], the INS will execute its order and deport him.'" *Id.,* at 939–940 (quoting *Chadha* v. *INS*, 634 F. 2d 408, 419 (CA9 1980)). This conclusion was not dictum. It was a necessary predicate to the Court's holding that "prior to Congress' intervention, there was adequate Art. III adverseness." 462 U. S., at 939. The holdings of cases are instructive, and the words of *Chadha* make clear its holding that the refusal of the Executive to provide the relief sought suffices to preserve a justiciable dispute as required by Article III. In short, even where "the Government largely agree[s] with the opposing party on the merits of the controversy," there is sufficient adverseness and an "adequate basis for jurisdiction in the fact that the Government intended to enforce the challenged law against that party." *Id.*, at 940, n. 12.

It is true that "[a] party who receives all that he has sought generally is not aggrieved by the judgment affording the relief and cannot appeal from it." *Roper, supra,* at 333, see also *Camreta* v. *Greene*, 563 U. S. ___, ___ (2011) (slip op., at 8) ("As a matter of practice and prudence, we have generally declined to consider cases at the request of a prevailing party, even when the Constitution allowed us to do so"). But this rule "does not have its source in the jurisdictional limitations of Art. III. In an appropriate case, appeal may be permitted . . . at the behest of the party who has prevailed on the merits, so long as that party retains a stake in the appeal satisfying the requirements of Art. III." *Roper, supra,* at 333–334.

While these principles suffice to show that this case presents a justiciable controversy under Article III, the prudential problems inherent in the Executive's unusual position require some further discussion. The Executive's agreement with Windsor's legal argument raises the risk that instead of a "'real, earnest and vital controversy,'" the Court faces a "friendly, non-adversary, proceeding . . . [in which] 'a party beaten in the legislature [seeks to] transfer to the courts an inquiry as to the constitutionality of the legislative act.'" *Ashwander* v. *TVA*, 297 U. S. 288, 346 (1936) (Brandeis, J., concurring) (quoting *Chicago & Grand Trunk R. Co.* v. *Wellman*, 143 U. S. 339, 345 (1892)). Even when Article III permits the exercise of federal jurisdiction, prudential considerations demand that the Court insist upon "that concrete adverseness which sharpens the presentation of issues upon which the court so largely depends for illumination of difficult constitutional questions." *Baker* v. *Carr*, 369 U. S. 186, 204 (1962).

There are, of course, reasons to hear a case and issue a ruling even when one party is reluctant to prevail in its position. Unlike Article III requirements—which must be satisfied by the parties before judicial consideration is appropriate—the relevant prudential factors that counsel against hearing this case are subject to "countervailing considerations [that] may outweigh the concerns underlying the usual reluctance to exert judicial power." *Warth*, 422 U. S., at 500–501. One consideration is the extent to which adversarial presentation of the issues is assured by the participation of *amici curiae* prepared to defend with vigor the constitutionality of the legislative act. With respect to this prudential aspect of standing as well, the *Chadha* Court encountered a similar situation. It noted that "there may be prudential, as opposed to Art. III, concerns about sanctioning the adjudication of [this case] in the absence of any participant supporting the validity of [the statute]. The Court of Appeals properly dispelled any such concerns by inviting and accepting briefs from both Houses of Congress." 462 U. S., at 940. *Chadha* was not an anomaly in this respect. The Court adopts the practice of entertaining arguments made by an *amicus* when the Solicitor General confesses error with respect to a judgment below, even if the confession is in effect an admission that an Act of Congress is unconstitutional. See, *e.g., Dickerson* v. *United States*, 530 U. S. 428 (2000).

In the case now before the Court the attorneys for BLAG present a substantial argument for the constitutionality of §3 of DOMA. BLAG's sharp adversarial presentation of the issues satisfies the prudential concerns that otherwise might counsel against hearing an appeal from a decision with which the principal parties agree. Were this Court to hold that prudential rules require it to dismiss the case, and, in consequence, that the Court of Appeals erred in failing to dismiss it as well, extensive litigation would ensue. The district courts in 94 districts throughout the Nation would be without precedential guidance not only in tax refund suits but also in cases involving the whole of DOMA's sweep involving over 1,000 federal statutes and a myriad of federal regulations. For instance, the opinion of the Court of Appeals for the First Circuit, addressing the validity of DOMA in a case involving regulations of the Department of Health and Human Services, likely would be vacated with instructions to dismiss, its ruling and guidance also then erased. See *Massachusetts* v. *United States Dept. of Health and Human Servs.*, 682 F. 3d 1 (CA1 2012). Rights and privileges of hundreds of thousands of persons would be adversely affected, pending a case in which all prudential concerns about justiciability are absent. That numerical prediction may not be certain, but it is certain that the cost in judicial resources and expense of litigation for all persons adversely affected would be immense. True, the very extent of DOMA's mandate means that at some point a case likely would arise without the prudential concerns raised here; but the costs, uncertainties, and alleged harm and injuries likely would continue for a time measured in years before the issue is resolved. In these unusual and urgent circumstances, the very term "prudential" counsels that it is a proper exercise of the Court's responsibility to take jurisdiction. For these reasons, the prudential and Article III requirements are met here; and, as a consequence, the Court need not decide whether BLAG would have standing to challenge the District Court's ruling and its affirmance in the Court of Appeals on BLAG's own authority.

The Court's conclusion that this petition may be heard on the merits does not imply that no difficulties would ensue if this were a common practice in ordinary cases. The Executive's failure to defend the constitutionality of an Act of Congress based on a constitutional theory not yet established in judicial decisions has created a procedural dilemma. On the one hand, as noted, the Government's agreement with Windsor raises questions about the propriety of entertaining a suit in which it seeks affirmance of an order invalidating a federal law and ordering the United States to pay money. On the other hand, if the Executive's agreement with a plaintiff that a law is unconsti- tutional is enough to preclude judicial review, then the Supreme Court's primary role in determining the constitutionality of a law that has inflicted real injury on a plaintiff who has brought a justiciable legal claim would become only secondary to the President's. This would undermine the clear dictate of the separation-of-powers principle that "when an Act of Congress is alleged to conflict with the Constitution, '[i]t is emphatically the province and duty of the judicial department to say what the law is.'" *Zivotofsky* v. *Clinton*, 566 U. S. ___, ___ (2012) (slip op., at 7) (quoting *Marbury* v. *Madison*, 1 Cranch 137, 177 (1803)). Similarly, with respect to the legislative power, when Congress has passed a statute and a President has signed it, it poses grave challenges to the separation of powers for the Executive at a particular moment to be able to nullify Congress' enactment solely on its own initiative and without any determination from the Court.

The Court's jurisdictional holding, it must be underscored, does not mean the arguments for dismissing this dispute on prudential grounds lack substance. Yet the difficulty the Executive faces should be acknowledged. When the Executive makes a principled determination that a statute is unconstitutional, it faces a difficult choice. Still, there is no suggestion here that it is appropriate for the Executive as a matter of course to challenge statutes in the judicial forum rather than making the case to Congress for their amendment or repeal. The integrity of the political process would be at risk if difficult constitutional issues were simply referred to the Court as a routine exercise. But this case is not routine. And the capable defense of the law by BLAG ensures that these prudential issues do not cloud the merits question, which is one of immediate importance to the Federal Government and to hundreds of thousands of persons. These circumstances support the Court's decision to proceed to the merits.

III

When at first Windsor and Spyer longed to marry, neither New York nor any other State granted them that right. After waiting some years, in 2007 they traveled to Ontario to be married there. It seems fair to conclude that, until recent years, many citizens had not even considered the possibility that two persons of the same sex might aspire to occupy the same status and dignity as that of a man and woman in lawful marriage. For marriage between a man and a woman no doubt had been thought of by most people as essential to the very definition of that term and to its role and function throughout the history of civilization. That belief, for many who long have held it, became even more urgent, more cherished when challenged. For others, however, came the beginnings of a new perspective, a new insight. Accordingly some States concluded that same-sex marriage ought to be given recognition and validity in the law for those same-sex couples who wish to define themselves by their commitment to each other. The limitation of lawful marriage to heterosexual couples, which for centuries had been deemed both necessary and fundamental, came to be seen in New York and certain other States as an unjust exclusion.

Slowly at first and then in rapid course, the laws of New York came to acknowledge the urgency of this issue for same-sex couples who wanted to affirm their commitment to one another before their children, their family, their friends, and their community. And so New York recognized same-sex marriages performed elsewhere; and then it later amended its own marriage laws to permit same-sex marriage. New York, in common with, as of this writing, 11 other States and the District of Columbia, decided that same-sex couples should have the right to marry and so live with pride in themselves and their union and in a status of equality with all other married persons. After a statewide deliberative process that enabled its citizens to discuss and weigh arguments for and against same-sex marriage, New York acted to enlarge the definition of marriage to correct what its citizens and elected representatives perceived to be an injustice that they had not earlier known or understood. See Marriage Equality Act, 2011 N. Y. Laws 749 (codified at N. Y. Dom. Rel. Law Ann. §§10–a, 10–b, 13 (West 2013)).

Against this background of lawful same-sex marriage in some States, the design, purpose, and effect of DOMA should be considered as the beginning point in deciding whether it is valid under the Constitution. By history and tradition the definition and regulation of marriage, as will be discussed in more detail, has been treated as being within the authority and realm of the separate States. Yet it is further established that Congress, in enacting discrete statutes, can make determinations that bear on marital rights and privileges. Just this Term the Court upheld the authority of the Congress to pre-empt state laws, allowing a former spouse to retain life insurance proceeds under a federal program that gave her priority, because of formal beneficiary designation rules, over the wife by a second marriage who survived the husband. *Hillman* v. *Maretta*, 569 U. S. ___ (2013); see also *Ridgway* v. *Ridgway*, 454 U. S. 46 (1981); *Wissner* v. *Wissner*, 338 U. S. 655 (1950). This is one example of the general principle that when the Federal Government acts in the exercise of its own proper authority, it has a wide choice of the mechanisms and means to adopt. See *McCulloch* v. *Maryland*, 4 Wheat. 316, 421 (1819). Congress has the power both to ensure efficiency in the administration of its programs and to choose what larger goals and policies to pursue.

Other precedents involving congressional statutes which affect marriages and family status further illustrate this point. In addressing the interaction of state domestic relations and federal immigration law Congress determined that marriages "entered into for the purpose of procuring an alien's admission [to the United States] as an immigrant" will not qualify the noncitizen for that status, even if the noncitizen's marriage is valid and proper for state-law purposes. 8 U. S. C. §1186a(b)(1) (2006 ed. and Supp. V). And in establishing income-based criteria for Social Security benefits, Congress decided that although state law would determine in general who qualifies as an applicant's spouse, common-law marriages also should be recognized, regardless of any particular State's view on these relationships. 42 U. S. C. §1382c(d)(2).

Though these discrete examples establish the constitutionality of limited federal laws that regulate the meaning of marriage in order to further federal policy, DOMA has a far greater reach; for it enacts a directive applicable to over 1,000 federal statutes and the whole realm of federal regulations. And its operation is directed to a class of persons that the laws of New York, and of 11 other States, have sought to protect. See *Goodridge* v. *Department of Public Health*, 440 Mass. 309, 798 N. E. 2d 941 (2003); An Act Implementing the Guarantee of Equal Protection Under the Constitution of the State for Same Sex Couples, 2009 Conn. Pub. Acts no. 09–13; *Varnum* v. *Brien*, 763 N. W. 2d 862 (Iowa 2009); Vt. Stat. Ann., Tit. 15, §8 (2010); N. H. Rev. Stat. Ann. §457:1–a (West Supp. 2012); Religious Freedom and Civil Marriage Equality Amendment Act of 2009, 57 D. C. Reg. 27 (Dec. 18, 2009); N. Y. Dom. Rel. Law Ann. §10–a (West Supp. 2013); Wash. Rev. Code §26.04.010 (2012); Citizen Initiative, Same- Sex Marriage, Question 1 (Me. 2012) (results online at http://www.maine.gov/sos/cec/elec/2012/tab-ref-2012.html (all Internet sources as visited June 18, 2013, and avail- able in Clerk of Court's case file)); Md. Fam. Law Code Ann. §2–201 (Lexis 2012); An Act to Amend Title 13 of the Delaware Code Relating to Domestic Relations to Provide for Same-Gender Civil Marriage and to Convert Existing Civil Unions to Civil

Marriages, 79 Del. Laws ch. 19 (2013); An act relating to marriage; providing for civil marriage between two persons; providing for exemptions and protections based on religious association, 2013 Minn. Laws ch. 74; An Act Relating to Domestic Relations— Persons Eligible to Marry, 2013 R. I. Laws ch. 4.

In order to assess the validity of that intervention it is necessary to discuss the extent of the state power and au- thority over marriage as a matter of history and tradi- tion. State laws defining and regulating marriage, of course, must respect the constitutional rights of persons, see*, e.g., Loving* v. *Virginia*, 388 U. S. 1 (1967); but, subject to those guarantees, "regulation of domestic relations" is "an area that has long been regarded as a virtually exclusive province of the States." *Sosna* v. *Iowa*, 419 U. S. 393, 404 (1975).

The recognition of civil marriages is central to state domestic relations law applicable to its residents and citizens. See *Williams* v. *North Carolina*, 317 U. S. 287, 298 (1942) ("Each state as a sovereign has a rightful and legitimate concern in the marital status of persons domiciled within its borders"). The definition of marriage is the foundation of the State's broader authority to regulate the subject of domestic relations with respect to the "[p]rotection of offspring, property interests, and the enforcement of marital responsibilities." *Ibid.* "[T]he states, at the time of the adoption of the Constitution, possessed full power over the subject of marriage and divorce . . . [and] the Constitution delegated no authority to the Government of the United States on the subject of marriage and divorce." *Haddock* v. *Haddock*, 201 U. S. 562, 575 (1906); see also *In re Burrus*, 136 U. S. 586, 593–594 (1890) ("The whole subject of the domestic relations of husband and wife, parent and child, belongs to the laws of the States and not to the laws of the United States").

Consistent with this allocation of authority, the Federal Government, through our history, has deferred to state-law policy decisions with respect to domestic relations. In *De Sylva* v. *Ballentine*, 351 U. S. 570 (1956), for example, the Court held that, "[t]o decide who is the widow or widower of a deceased author, or who are his executors or next of kin," under the Copyright Act "requires a reference to the law of the State which created those legal relationships" because "there is no federal law of domestic relations." *Id.,* at 580. In order to respect this principle, the federal courts, as a general rule, do not adjudicate issues of marital status even when there might otherwise be a basis for federal jurisdiction. See *Ankenbrandt* v. *Richards*, 504 U. S. 689, 703 (1992). Federal courts will not hear divorce and custody cases even if they arise in diversity because of "the virtually exclusive primacy . . . of the States in the regulation of domestic relations." *Id.,* at 714 (Blackmun, J., concurring in judgment).

The significance of state responsibilities for the definition and regulation of marriage dates to the Nation's beginning; for "when the Constitution was adopted the common understanding was that the domestic relations of husband and wife and parent and child were matters reserved to the States." *Ohio ex rel. Popovici* v. *Agler*, 280 U. S. 379, 383–384 (1930). Marriage laws vary in some respects from State to State. For example, the required minimum age is 16 in Vermont, but only 13 in New Hampshire. Compare Vt. Stat. Ann., Tit. 18, §5142 (2012), with N. H. Rev. Stat. Ann. §457:4 (West Supp. 2012). Likewise the permissible degree of consanguinity can vary (most States permit first cousins to marry, but a handful— such as Iowa and Washington, see Iowa Code §595.19 (2009); Wash. Rev. Code §26.04.020 (2012)—prohibit the practice). But these rules are in every event consistent within each State.

Against this background DOMA rejects the long-established precept that the incidents, benefits, and obligations of marriage are uniform for all married couples within each State, though they may vary, subject to constitutional guarantees, from one State to the next. Despite these considerations, it is unnecessary to decide whether this federal intrusion on state power is a violation of the Constitution because it disrupts the federal balance. The State's power in defining the marital relation is of central relevance in this case quite apart from principles of federalism. Here the State's decision to give this class of persons the right to marry conferred upon them a dignity and status of immense import. When the State used its historic and essential authority to define the marital relation in this way, its role and its power in making the decision enhanced the recognition, dignity, and protection of the class in their own community. DOMA, because of its reach and extent, departs from this history and tra- dition of reliance on state law to define marriage. "'[D]iscriminations of an unusual character especially suggest careful consideration to determine whether they are obnoxious to the constitutional provision.'" *Romer* v. *Evans*, 517 U. S. 620, 633 (1996) (quoting *Louisville Gas & Elec. Co.* v. *Coleman*, 277 U. S. 32, 37–38 (1928)).

The Federal Government uses this state-defined class for the opposite purpose—to impose restrictions and dis- abilities. That result requires this Court now to address whether the resulting injury and indignity is a deprivation of an essential part of the liberty protected by the Fifth Amendment. What the State of New York treats as alike the federal law deems unlike by a law designed to injure the same class the State seeks to protect.

In acting first to recognize and then to allow same-sex marriages, New York was responding “to the initiative of those who [sought] a voice in shaping the destiny of their own times.” *Bond* v. *United States*, 564 U. S. ___, ___ (2011) (slip op., at 9). These actions were without doubt a proper exercise of its sovereign authority within our fed- eral system, all in the way that the Framers of the Constitution intended. The dynamics of state government in the federal system are to allow the formation of consensus respecting the way the members of a discrete community treat each other in their daily contact and constant interaction with each other.

The States’ interest in defining and regulating the marital relation, subject to constitutional guarantees, stems from the understanding that marriage is more than a routine classification for purposes of certain statutory benefits. Private, consensual sexual intimacy between two adult persons of the same sex may not be punished by the State, and it can form “but one element in a personal bond that is more enduring.” *Lawrence* v. *Texas*, 539 U. S. 558, 567 (2003). By its recognition of the validity of same-sex marriages performed in other jurisdictions and then by authorizing same-sex unions and same-sex marriages, New York sought to give further protection and dignity to that bond. For same-sex couples who wished to be married, the State acted to give their lawful conduct a lawful status. This status is a far-reaching legal acknowledgment of the intimate relationship between two people, a relationship deemed by the State worthy of dignity in the community equal with all other marriages. It reflects both the community’s considered perspective on the historical roots of the institution of marriage and its evolving understanding of the meaning of equality.

IV

DOMA seeks to injure the very class New York seeks to protect. By doing so it violates basic due process and equal protection principles applicable to the Federal Government. See U. S. Const., Amdt. 5; *Bolling* v. *Sharpe*, 347 U. S. 497 (1954). The Constitution’s guarantee of equality “must at the very least mean that a bare con- gressional desire to harm a politically unpopular group cannot” justify disparate treatment of that group. *Department of Agriculture* v. *Moreno*, 413 U. S. 528, 534–535 (1973). In determining whether a law is motived by an improper animus or purpose, “‘[d]iscriminations of an un- usual character’” especially require careful consideration. *Supra,* at 19 (quoting *Romer*, *supra*, at 633). DOMA cannot survive under these principles. The responsibility of the States for the regulation of domestic relations is an important indicator of the substantial societal impact the State's classifications have in the daily lives and customs of its people. DOMA's unusual deviation from the usual tradition of recognizing and accepting state definitions of marriage here operates to deprive same-sex couples of the benefits and responsibilities that come with the federal recognition of their marriages. This is strong evidence of a law having the purpose and effect of disapproval of that class. The avowed purpose and practical effect of the law here in question are to impose a disadvantage, a separate status, and so a stigma upon all who enter into same-sex marriages made lawful by the unquestioned authority of the States.

The history of DOMA's enactment and its own text demonstrate that interference with the equal dignity of same-sex marriages, a dignity conferred by the States in the exercise of their sovereign power, was more than an incidental effect of the federal statute. It was its essence. The House Report announced its conclusion that "it is both appropriate and necessary for Congress to do what it can to defend the institution of traditional heterosexual marriage. . . . H. R. 3396 is appropriately entitled the 'Defense of Marriage Act.' The effort to redefine 'marriage' to extend to homosexual couples is a truly radical proposal that would fundamentally alter the institution of marriage." H. R. Rep. No. 104–664, pp. 12–13 (1996). The House concluded that DOMA expresses "both moral disapproval of homosexuality, and a moral conviction that heterosexuality better comports with traditional (especially Judeo-Christian) morality." *Id.,* at 16 (footnote deleted). The stated purpose of the law was to promote an "interest in protecting the traditional moral teachings reflected in heterosexual-only marriage laws." *Ibid.* Were there any doubt of this far-reaching purpose, the title of the Act confirms it: The Defense of Marriage.

The arguments put forward by BLAG are just as candid about the congressional purpose to influence or interfere with state sovereign choices about who may be married. As the title and dynamics of the bill indicate, its purpose is to discourage enactment of state same-sex marriage laws and to restrict the freedom and choice of couples married under those laws if they are enacted. The congressional goal was "to put a thumb on the scales and influence a state's decision as to how to shape its own marriage laws." *Massachusetts*, 682 F. 3d, at 12–13. The Act's demonstrated purpose is to ensure that if any State decides to recognize same-sex marriages, those unions will be treated as second-class marriages for purposes of federal law. This raises a most serious question under the Constitution's Fifth Amendment.

DOMA's operation in practice confirms this purpose. When New York adopted a law to permit same-sex marriage, it sought to eliminate inequality; but DOMA frustrates that objective through a system-wide enactment with no identified connection to any particular area of fed- eral law. DOMA writes inequality into the entire United States Code. The particular case at hand concerns the estate tax, but DOMA is more than a simple determination of what should or should not be allowed as an estate tax refund. Among the over 1,000 statutes and numerous federal regulations that DOMA controls are laws pertaining to Social Security, housing, taxes, criminal sanctions, copyright, and veterans' benefits.

DOMA's principal effect is to identify a subset of state-sanctioned marriages and make them unequal. The principal purpose is to impose inequality, not for other reasons like governmental efficiency. Responsibilities, as well as rights, enhance the dignity and integrity of the person. And DOMA contrives to deprive some couples married under the laws of their State, but not other couples, of both rights and responsibilities. By creating two contradictory marriage regimes within the same State, DOMA forces same-sex couples to live as married for the purpose of state law but unmarried for the purpose of federal law, thus diminishing the stability and predictability of basic personal relations the State has found it proper to acknowledge and protect. By this dynamic DOMA undermines both the public and private significance of state-sanctioned same-sex marriages; for it tells those couples, and all the world, that their otherwise valid marriages are unworthy of federal recognition. This places same-sex couples in an unstable position of being in a second-tier marriage. The differentiation demeans the couple, whose moral and sexual choices the Constitution protects, see *Lawrence*, 539 U. S. 558, and whose relationship the State has sought to dignify. And it humiliates tens of thousands of children now being raised by same-sex couples. The law in question makes it even more difficult for the children to understand the integrity and closeness of their own family and its concord with other families in their community and in their daily lives.

Under DOMA, same-sex married couples have their lives burdened, by reason of government decree, in visible and public ways. By its great reach, DOMA touches many aspects of married and family life, from the mundane to the profound. It prevents same-sex married couples from obtaining government healthcare benefits they would otherwise receive. See 5 U. S. C. §§8901(5), 8905. It deprives them of the Bankruptcy Code's special protections for domestic-support obligations. See 11 U. S. C. §§101(14A), 507(a)(1)(A), 523(a)(5), 523(a)(15). It forces them to follow a complicated procedure to file their state and federal taxes jointly. Technical Bulletin TB–55, 2010 Vt. Tax LEXIS 6 (Oct. 7, 2010); Brief for Federalism Scholars as *Amici Curiae* 34. It prohibits them from being buried together in veterans' cemeteries. National Cemetery Administration Directive 3210/1, p. 37 (June 4, 2008).

For certain married couples, DOMA's unequal effects are even more serious. The federal penal code makes it a crime to "assaul[t], kidna[p], or murde[r] . . . a member of the immediate family" of "a United States official, a United States judge, [or] a Federal law enforcement officer," 18 U. S. C. §115(a)(1)(A), with the intent to influence or retaliate against that official, §115(a)(1). Although a "spouse" qualifies as a member of the officer's "immediate family," §115(c)(2), DOMA makes this protection inapplicable to same-sex spouses.

DOMA also brings financial harm to children of same-sex couples. It raises the cost of health care for families by taxing health benefits provided by employers to their workers' same-sex spouses. See 26 U. S. C. §106; Treas. Reg. §1.106–1, 26 CFR §1.106–1 (2012); IRS Private Letter Ruling 9850011 (Sept. 10, 1998). And it denies or re- duces benefits allowed to families upon the loss of a spouse and parent, benefits that are an integral part of family security. See Social Security Administration, Social Security Survivors Benefits 5 (2012) (benefits available to a surviving spouse caring for the couple's child), online at http://www.ssa.gov/pubs/EN-05-10084.pdf.

DOMA divests married same-sex couples of the duties and responsibilities that are an essential part of married life and that they in most cases would be honored to accept were DOMA not in force. For instance, because it is expected that spouses will support each other as they pursue educational opportunities, federal law takes into consideration a spouse's income in calculating a student's fed- eral financial aid eligibility. See 20 U. S. C. §1087nn(b). Same-sex married couples are exempt from this requirement. The same is true with respect to federal ethics rules. Federal executive and agency officials are prohibited from "participat[ing] personally and substantially" in matters as to which they or their spouses have a financial interest. 18 U. S. C. §208(a). A similar statute prohibits Senators, Senate employees, and their spouses from accepting high-value gifts from certain sources, see 2 U. S. C. §31–2(a)(1), and another mandates detailed financial disclosures by numerous high-ranking officials and their spouses. See 5 U. S. C. App. §§102(a), (e). Under DOMA, however, these Government-integrity rules do not apply to same-sex spouses.

* * *

The power the Constitution grants it also restrains. And though Congress has great authority to design laws to fit its own conception of sound national policy, it cannot deny the liberty protected by the Due Process Clause of the Fifth Amendment.

What has been explained to this point should more than suffice to establish that the principal purpose and the necessary effect of this law are to demean those persons who are in a lawful same-sex marriage. This requires the Court to hold, as it now does, that DOMA is unconstitutional as a deprivation of the liberty of the person protected by the Fifth Amendment of the Constitution.

The liberty protected by the Fifth Amendment's Due Process Clause contains within it the prohibition against denying to any person the equal protection of the laws. See *Bolling*, 347 U. S., at 499–500; *Adarand Constructors, Inc.* v. *Peña*, 515 U. S. 200, 217–218 (1995). While the Fifth Amendment itself withdraws from Government the power to degrade or demean in the way this law does, the equal protection guarantee of the Fourteenth Amendment makes that Fifth Amendment right all the more specific and all the better understood and preserved.

The class to which DOMA directs its restrictions and restraints are those persons who are joined in same-sex marriages made lawful by the State. DOMA singles out a class of persons deemed by a State entitled to recognition and protection to enhance their own liberty. It imposes a disability on the class by refusing to acknowledge a status the State finds to be dignified and proper. DOMA instructs all federal officials, and indeed all persons with whom same-sex couples interact, including their own children, that their marriage is less worthy than the marriages of others. The federal statute is invalid, for no legitimate purpose overcomes the purpose and effect to disparage and to injure those whom the State, by its marriage laws, sought to protect in personhood and dignity. By seeking to displace this protection and treating those persons as living in marriages less respected than others, the federal statute is in violation of the Fifth Amendment. This opinion and its holding are confined to those lawful marriages.

The judgment of the Court of Appeals for the Second Circuit is affirmed.

It is so ordered.

ROBERTS, C. J., dissenting

SUPREME COURT OF THE UNITED STATES

No. 12–307

UNITED STATES, PETITIONER *v.* EDITH SCHLAIN WINDSOR, IN HER CAPACITY AS EXECUTOR OF THE ESTATE OF THEA CLARA SPYER, ET AL.

ON WRIT OF CERTIORARI TO THE UNITED STATES COURT OF APPEALS FOR THE SECOND CIRCUIT

[June 26, 2013]

CHIEF JUSTICE ROBERTS, dissenting.

I agree with JUSTICE SCALIA that this Court lacks jurisdiction to review the decisions of the courts below. On the merits of the constitutional dispute the Court decides to decide, I also agree with JUSTICE SCALIA that Congress acted constitutionally in passing the Defense of Marriage Act (DOMA). Interests in uniformity and stability am- ply justified Congress's decision to retain the definition of marriage that, at that point, had been adopted by every State in our Nation, and every nation in the world. *Post*, at 19–20 (dissenting opinion).

The majority sees a more sinister motive, pointing out that the Federal Government has generally (though not uniformly) deferred to state definitions of marriage in the past. That is true, of course, but none of those prior stateby-state variations had involved differences over something—as the majority puts it—"thought of by most people as essential to the very definition of [marriage] and to its role and function throughout the history of civilization." *Ante*, at 13. That the Federal Government treated this fundamental question differently than it treated variations over consanguinity or minimum age is hardly surprising— and hardly enough to support a conclusion that the "principal purpose," *ante*, at 22, of the 342 Representatives and 85 Senators who voted for it, and the President who signed it, was a bare desire to harm. Nor do the snip- pets of legislative history and the banal title of the Act to which the majority points suffice to make such a showing. At least without some more convincing evidence that the Act's principal purpose was to codify malice, and that it furthered *no* legitimate government interests, I would not tar the political branches with the brush of bigotry.

But while I disagree with the result to which the majority's analysis leads it in this case, I think it more important to point out that its analysis leads no further. The Court does not have before it, and the logic of its opinion does not decide, the distinct question whether the States, in the exercise of their "historic and essential authority to define the marital relation," *ante*, at 18, may continue to utilize the traditional definition of marriage.

The majority goes out of its way to make this explicit in the penultimate sentence of its opinion. It states that "[t]his opinion and its holding are confined to those lawful marriages," *ante*, at 26—referring to same-sex marriages that a State has already recognized as a result of the local "community's considered perspective on the historical roots of the institution of marriage and its evolving un- derstanding of the meaning of equality." *Ante,* at 20. JUSTICE SCALIA believes this is a "'bald, unreasoned disclaime[r].'" *Post*, at 22. In my view, though, the disclaimer is a logical and necessary consequence of the argument the majority has chosen to adopt. The dominant theme of the majority opinion is that the Federal Government's intrusion into an area "central to state domestic relations law applicable to its residents and citizens" is sufficiently "unusual" to set off alarm bells. *Ante*, at 17, 20. I think the majority goes off course, as I have said, but it is undeniable that its judgment is based on federalism.

The majority extensively chronicles DOMA's departure from the normal allocation of responsibility between State and Federal Governments, emphasizing that DOMA "rejects the long-established precept that the incidents, benefits, and obligations of marriage are uniform for all married couples within each State." *Ante,* at 18. But there is no such departure when one State adopts or keeps a definition of marriage that differs from that of its neighbor, for it is entirely expected that state definitions would "vary, subject to constitutional guarantees, from one State to the next." *Ibid*. Thus, while "[t]he State's power in defining the marital relation is of central relevance" to the majority's decision to strike down DOMA here, *ibid.*, that power will come into play on the other side of the board in future cases about the constitutionality of state marriage definitions. So too will the concerns for state diversity and sovereignty that weigh against DOMA's constitutionality in this case. See *ante,* at 19.

It is not just this central feature of the majority's analysis that is unique to DOMA, but many considerations on the periphery as well. For example, the majority focuses on the legislative history and title of this particular Act, *ante*, at 21; those statute-specific considerations will, of course, be irrelevant in future cases about different statutes. The majority emphasizes that DOMA was a "system- wide enactment with no identified connection to any particular area of federal law," but a State's definition of marriage "is the foundation of the

State's broader author- ity to regulate the subject of domestic relations with respect to the '[p]rotection of offspring, property interests, and the enforcement of marital responsibilities.'" *Ante*, at 22, 17. And the federal decision undermined (in the majority's view) the "dignity [already] conferred by the States in the exercise of their sovereign power," *ante*, at 21, whereas a State's decision whether to expand the definition of marriage from its traditional contours involves no similar concern.

We may in the future have to resolve challenges to state marriage definitions affecting same-sex couples. That issue, however, is not before us in this case, and we hold today that we lack jurisdiction to consider it in the particular context of *Hollingsworth* v. *Perry*, *ante,* p. ___. I write only to highlight the limits of the majority's holding and reasoning today, lest its opinion be taken to resolve not only a question that I believe is not properly before us— DOMA's constitutionality—but also a question that all agree, and the Court explicitly acknowledges, is not at issue.

SCALIA, J., dissenting

SUPREME COURT OF THE UNITED STATES

No. 12–307

UNITED STATES, PETITIONER *v.* EDITH SCHLAIN WINDSOR, IN HER CAPACITY AS EXECUTOR OF THE ESTATE OF THEA CLARA SPYER, ET AL.

ON WRIT OF CERTIORARI TO THE UNITED STATES COURT OF APPEALS FOR THE SECOND CIRCUIT

[June 26, 2013]

JUSTICE SCALIA, with whom JUSTICE THOMAS joins, and with whom THE CHIEF JUSTICE joins as to Part I, dissenting.

This case is about power in several respects. It is about the power of our people to govern themselves, and the power of this Court to pronounce the law. Today's opinion aggrandizes the latter, with the predictable consequence of diminishing the former. We have no power to decide this case. And even if we did, we have no power under the Constitution to invalidate this democratically adopted leg- islation. The Court's errors on both points spring forth from the same diseased root: an exalted conception of the role of this institution in America.

I

A

The Court is eager—*hungry*—to tell everyone its view of the legal question at the heart of this case. Standing in the way is an obstacle, a technicality of little interest to anyone but the people of We the People, who created it as a barrier against judges' intrusion into their lives. They gave judges, in Article III, only the "judicial Power," a power to decide not abstract questions but real, concrete "Cases" and "Controversies." Yet the plaintiff and the Government agree entirely on what should happen in this lawsuit. They agree that the court below got it right; and they agreed in the court below that the court below that one got it right as well. What, then, are we *doing* here?

The answer lies at the heart of the jurisdictional portion of today's opinion, where a single sentence lays bare the majority's vision of our role. The Court says that we have the power to decide this case because if we did not, then our "primary role in determining the constitutionality of a law" (at least one that "has inflicted real injury on a plaintiff ") would "become only secondary to the President's." *Ante,* at 12. But wait, the reader wonders—Windsor won below, and so *cured* her injury, and the President was glad to see it. True, says the majority, but judicial review must march on regardless, lest we "undermine the clear dictate of the separation-of-powers principle that when an Act of Congress is alleged to conflict with the Constitution, it is emphatically the province and duty of the judicial department to say what the law is." *Ibid.* (internal quotation marks and brackets omitted).

That is jaw-dropping. It is an assertion of judicial supremacy over the people's Representatives in Congress and the Executive. It envisions a Supreme Court standing (or rather enthroned) at the apex of government, empowered to decide all constitutional questions, always and every- where "primary" in its role.

This image of the Court would have been unrecognizable to those who wrote and ratified our national charter. They knew well the dangers of "primary" power, and so created branches of government that would be "perfectly coordinate by the terms of their common commission," none of which branches could "pretend to an exclusive or superior right of settling the boundaries between their respective powers." The Federalist, No. 49, p. 314 (C. Rossiter ed. 1961) (J. Madison). The people did this to protect themselves. They did it to guard their right to self-rule against the black-robed supremacy that today's majority finds so attractive. So it was that Madison could confidently state, with no fear of contradiction, that there was nothing of "greater intrinsic value" or "stamped with the authority of more enlightened patrons of liberty" than a government of separate and coordinate powers. *Id.*, No. 47, at 301.

For this reason we are quite forbidden to say what the law is whenever (as today's opinion asserts) "'an Act of Congress is alleged to conflict with the Constitution.'" *Ante*, at 12. We can do so only when that allegation will determine the outcome of a lawsuit, and is contradicted by the other party. The "judicial Power" is not, as the majority believes, the power "'to say what the law is,'" *ibid.,* giving the Supreme Court the "primary role in determining the constitutionality of laws." The majority must have in mind one of the foreign constitutions that pronounces such primacy for its constitutional court and allows that primacy to be exercised in contexts other than a lawsuit. See, *e.g.,* Basic Law for the Federal Republic of Germany, Art. 93. The judicial power as Americans have understood it (and their English ancestors before them) is the power to adjudicate, with conclusive effect, disputed government claims (civil or criminal) against private persons, and disputed claims by private persons against the government or other private persons. Sometimes (though not always) the parties before the court disagree not with regard to the facts of their case (or not *only* with regard to the facts) but with regard to the applicable law—in which event (and *only* in which event) it becomes the "'province and duty of the judicial department to say what the law is.'" *Ante*, at 12.

In other words, declaring the compatibility of state or federal laws with the Constitution is not only not the "primary role" of this Court, it is not a separate, free-standing role *at all.* We perform that role incidentally—by accident, as it were—when that is necessary to resolve the dispute before us. Then, and only then, does it become "'the province and duty of the judicial department to say what the law is.'" That is why, in 1793, we politely declined the Washington Administration's request to "say what the law is" on a particular treaty matter that was not the subject of a concrete legal controversy. 3 Correspondence and Public Papers of John Jay 486–489 (H. Johnston ed. 1893). And that is why, as our opinions have said, some questions of law will *never* be presented to this Court, because there will never be anyone with standing to bring a lawsuit. See *Schlesinger* v. *Reservists Comm. to Stop the War*, 418 U. S. 208, 227 (1974); *United States* v. *Richardson*, 418 U. S. 166, 179 (1974). As Justice Bran- deis put it, we cannot "pass upon the constitutionality of legislation in a friendly, non-adversary, proceeding"; ab-sent a "'real, earnest and vital controversy between individuals,'" we have neither any work to do nor any power to do it. *Ashwander* v. *TVA*, 297 U. S. 288, 346 (1936) (concurring opinion) (quoting *Chicago & Grand Trunk R. Co.* v. *Wellman*, 143 U. S. 339, 345 (1892)). Our authority begins and ends with the need to adjudge the rights of an injured party who stands before us seeking redress. *Lujan* v. *Defenders of Wildlife*, 504 U. S. 555, 560 (1992).

That is completely absent here. Windsor's injury was cured by the judgment in her favor. And while, in ordinary circumstances, the United States is injured by a directive to pay a tax refund, this suit is far from ordinary. Whatever injury the United States has suffered will surely not be redressed by the action that it, as a litigant, asks us to take. The final sentence of the Solicitor General's brief on the merits reads: "For the foregoing reasons, the judgment of the court of appeals *should be affirmed*." Brief for United States (merits) 54 (emphasis added). That will not cure the Government's injury, but carve it into stone. One could spend many fruitless afternoons ransacking our library for any other petitioner's brief seeking an affirmance of the judgment against it.[1] What the petitioner United States asks us to do in the case before us is exactly what the respondent Windsor asks us to do: not to provide relief from the judgment below but to say that that judgment was correct. And the same was true in the Court of Appeals: Neither party sought to undo the judgment for Windsor, and so that court should have dismissed the appeal (just as we should dismiss) for lack of jurisdiction. Since both parties agreed with the judgment of the District Court for the Southern District of New York, the suit should have ended there. The further proceedings have been a contrivance, having no object in mind except to ele- vate a District Court judgment that has no precedential effect in other courts, to one that has precedential effect throughout the Second Circuit, and then (in this Court) precedential effect throughout the United States.

We have never before agreed to speak—to "say what the law is"—where there is no controversy before us. In the more than two centuries that this Court has existed as an institution, we have never suggested that we have the power to decide a question when every party agrees with both its nominal opponent *and the court below* on that question's answer. The United States reluctantly conceded that at oral argument. See Tr. of Oral Arg. 19–20.

The closest we have ever come to what the Court blesses today was our opinion in *INS* v. *Chadha*, 462 U. S. 919 (1983). But in that case, two parties to the litigation disagreed with the position of the United States and with the court below: the House and Senate, which had intervened in the case. Because *Chadha* concerned the validity of a mode of congressional action—the one-house legis- lative veto—the House and Senate were threatened with destruction of what they claimed to be one of their institutional powers. The Executive choosing not to defend that power,[2] we permitted the House and Senate to intervene. Nothing like that is present here.

To be sure, the Court in *Chadha* said that statutory aggrieved-party status was "not altered by the fact that the Executive may agree with the holding that the statute in question is unconstitutional." *Id.*, at 930–931. But in a footnote to that statement, the Court acknowledged Arti- cle III's separate requirement of a "justiciable case or controversy," and stated that *this* requirement was satisfied "because of the presence of the two Houses of Congress as adverse parties." *Id.,* at 931, n. 6. Later in its opinion, the *Chadha* Court remarked that the United States' announced intention to enforce the statute also sufficed to permit judicial review, even absent congressional participation. *Id.,* at 939. That remark is true, as a description of the judicial review conducted in the Court of Appeals, where the Houses of Congress had not intervened. (The case originated in the Court of Appeals, since it sought review of agency action under 8 U. S. C. §1105a(a) (1976 ed.).) There, absent a judgment setting aside the INS order, Chadha faced deportation. This passage of our opinion seems to be addressing that initial standing in the Court of Appeals, as indicated by its quotation from the lower court's opinion, 462 U. S., at 939– 940. But if it was addressing standing to pursue the appeal, the remark was both the purest dictum (as congressional intervention at that point made the required adverseness "beyond doubt," *id.*, at 939), and quite incorrect. When a private party has a judicial decree safely in hand to prevent his injury, additional judicial action requires that a party injured by the decree *seek to undo it*. In *Chadha*, the intervening House and Senate fulfilled that requirement. Here no one does.

The majority's discussion of the requirements of Article III bears no resemblance to our jurisprudence. It accuses the *amicus* (appointed to argue against our jurisdiction) of "elid[ing] the distinction between . . . the jurisdictional requirements of Article III and the prudential limits on its exercise." *Ante*, at 6. It then proceeds to call the requirement of adverseness a "prudential" aspect of standing. *Of standing.* That is incomprehensible. A plaintiff (or appellant) can have all the standing in the world—satisfying all three standing requirements of *Lujan* that the majority so carefully quotes, *ante,* at 7—and yet no Article III controversy may be before the court. Article III requires not just a plaintiff (or appellant) who has standing to complain but *an opposing party* who denies the validity of the complaint. It is not the *amicus* that has done the eliding of distinctions, but the majority, calling the quite separate Article III requirement of adverseness between the parties an element (which it then pronounces a "prudential" element) of standing. The question here is not whether, as the majority puts it, "the United States retains a stake sufficient to support Article III jurisdiction," *ibid.* the question is whether there is any controversy (which requires *contradiction*) between the United States and Ms. Windsor. There is not.

I find it wryly amusing that the majority seeks to dismiss the requirement of party-adverseness as nothing more than a "prudential" aspect of the sole Article III requirement of standing. (Relegating a jurisdictional requirement to "prudential" status is a wondrous device, enabling courts to ignore the requirement whenever they believe it "prudent"—which is to say, a good idea.) Half a century ago, a Court similarly bent upon announcing its view regarding the constitutionality of a federal statute achieved that goal by effecting a remarkably similar *but completely opposite* distortion of the principles limiting our jurisdiction. The Court's notorious opinion in *Flast* v. *Cohen*, 392 U. S. 83, 98–101 (1968), held that *standing* was merely an element (which it pronounced to be a "prudential" element) of the sole Article III requirement of *adverseness*. We have been living with the chaos created by that power-grabbing decision ever since, see *Hein* v. *Freedom From Religion Foundation, Inc.*, 551 U. S. 587 (2007), as we will have to live with the chaos created by this one.

The authorities the majority cites fall miles short of supporting the counterintuitive notion that an Article III "controversy" can exist without disagreement between the parties. In *Deposit Guaranty Nat. Bank* v. *Roper*, 445 U. S. 326 (1980), the District Court had entered judgment in the individual plaintiff 's favor based on the defendant bank's offer to pay the full amount claimed. The plaintiff, however, sought to appeal the District Court's denial of class certification under Federal Rule of Civil Procedure 23. There was a continuing dispute between the parties concerning the issue raised on appeal. The same is true of the other case cited by the majority, *Camreta* v. *Greene*, 563 U. S. ___ (2011). There the District Court found that the defendant state officers had violated the Fourth Amendment, but rendered judgment in their favor because they were entitled to official immunity, application of the Fourth Amendment to their conduct not having been clear at the time of violation. The officers sought to appeal the holding of Fourth Amendment violation, which would circumscribe their future conduct; the plaintiff continued to insist that a Fourth Amendment violation had occurred. The "prudential" discretion to which both those cases refer was the discretion to *deny* an appeal even when a live controversy exists—not the discretion to *grant* one when it does not. The majority can cite no case in which this Court entertained an appeal in which both parties urged us to affirm the judgment below. And that is because the existence of a controversy is not a "prudential" requirement that we have invented, but an essential element of an Article III case or controversy. The majority's notion that a case between friendly parties can be entertained so long as "adversarial presentation of the issues is assured by the participation of *amici curiae* prepared to defend with vigor" the other side of the issue, *ante*, at 10, effects a breathtaking revolution in our Article III jurisprudence.

It may be argued that if what we say is true some Presidential determinations that statutes are unconstitutional will not be subject to our review. That is as it should be, when both the President and the plaintiff agree that the statute is unconstitutional. Where the Executive is en- forcing an unconstitutional law, suit will of course lie; but if, in that suit, the Executive admits the unconstitution- ality of the law, the litigation should end in an order or a consent decree enjoining enforcement. This suit saw the light of day only because the President enforced the Act (and thus gave Windsor standing to sue) even though he believed it unconstitutional. He could have equally chosen (more appropriately, some would say) neither to enforce nor to defend the statute he believed to be unconstitu- tional, see Presidential Authority to Decline to Execute Un- constitutional Statutes, 18 Op. Off. Legal Counsel 199 (Nov. 2, 1994)—in which event Windsor would not have been injured, the District Court could not have refereed this friendly scrimmage, and the Executive's determination of unconstitutionality would have escaped this Court's desire to blurt out its view of the law. The matter would have been left, as so many matters ought to be left, to a tug of war between the President and the Congress, which has innumerable means (up to and including impeachment) of compelling the President to enforce the laws it has written. Or the President could have evaded presentation of the constitutional issue to this Court simply by declining to appeal the District Court and Court of Appeals dispositions he agreed with. Be sure of this much: If a President wants to insulate his judgment of unconstitutionality from our review, he can. What the views urged in this dissent produce is not insulation from judicial review but insulation from Executive contrivance.

The majority brandishes the famous sentence from *Marbury* v. *Madison*, 1 Cranch 137, 177 (1803) that "[i]t is emphatically the province and duty of the judicial department to say what the law is." *Ante*, at 12 (internal quotation marks omitted). But that sentence neither says nor implies that it is *always* the province and duty of the Court to say what the law is—much less that its responsibility in that regard is a "primary" one. The very next sentence of Chief Justice Marshall's opinion makes the crucial qualification that today's majority ignores: "*Those who apply the rule to particular cases*, must of necessity expound and interpret that rule." 1 Cranch, at 177 (emphasis added). Only when a "particular case" is before us—that is, a controversy that it is our business to resolve under Article III—do we have the province and duty to pronounce the law. For the views of our early Court more precisely addressing the question before us here, the ma- jority ought instead to have consulted the opinion of Chief Justice Taney in *Lord* v. *Veazie*, 8 How. 251 (1850):

> "The objection in the case before us is . . . that the plaintiff and defendant have the same interest, and that interest adverse and in conflict with the interest of third persons, whose rights would be seriously affected if the question of law was decided in the manner that both of the parties to this suit desire it to be.
>
> "A judgment entered under such circumstances, and for such purposes, is a mere form. The whole proceeding was in contempt of the court, and highly reprehensible . . . . A judgment in form, thus procured, in the eye of the law is no judgment of the court. It is a nullity, and no writ of error will lie upon it. This writ is, therefore, dismissed." *Id.,* at 255–256.

There is, in the words of *Marbury,* no "necessity [to] expound and interpret" the law in this case; just a desire to place this Court at the center of the Nation's life. 1 Cranch, at 177.

B

A few words in response to the theory of jurisdiction set forth in JUSTICE ALITO's dissent: Though less far reaching in its consequences than the majority's conversion of constitutionally required adverseness into a discretionary element of standing, the theory of that dissent similarly elevates the Court to the "primary" determiner of constitutional questions involving the separation of powers, and, to boot, increases the power of the most dangerous branch: the "legislative department," which by its nature "draw[s] all power into its impetuous vortex." The Federalist, No. 48, at 309 (J. Madison). Heretofore in our national history, the President's failure to "take Care that the Laws be faithfully executed," U. S. Const., Art. II, §3, could only be brought before a judicial tribunal by someone whose concrete interests were harmed by that alleged failure. JUSTICE ALITO would create a system in which Congress can hale the Executive before the courts not only to vindicate its own institutional powers to act, but to correct a perceived inadequacy in the execution of its laws.[3] This would lay to rest Tocqueville's praise of our judicial system as one which "intimately bind[s] the case made for the law with the case made for one man," one in which legislation is "no longer exposed to the daily aggression of the parties," and in which "[t]he political question that [the judge] must resolve is linked to the interest" of private litigants. A. de Tocqueville, Democracy in America 97 (H. Mansfield & D. Winthrop eds. 2000). That would be replaced by a system in which Congress and the Executive can pop immediately into court, in their institutional capacity, whenever the President refuses to implement a statute he believes to be unconstitutional, and whenever he implements a law in a manner that is not to Congress's liking.

JUSTICE ALITO's notion of standing will likewise enormously shrink the area to which "judicial censure, exercised by the courts on legislation, cannot extend," *ibid.* For example, a bare majority of both Houses could bring into court the assertion that the Executive's implementation of welfare programs is too generous—a failure that no other litigant would have standing to complain about. Moreover, as we indicated in *Raines* v. *Byrd*, 521 U. S. 811, 828 (1997), if Congress can sue the Executive for the erroneous application of the law that "injures" its power to legislate, surely the Executive can sue Congress for its erroneous adoption of an unconstitutional law that "injures" the Executive's power to administer—or perhaps for its protracted failure to act on one of his nominations. The opportunities for dragging the courts into disputes hith- erto left for political resolution are endless.

JUSTICE ALITO's dissent is correct that *Raines* did not formally decide this issue, but its reasoning does. The opinion spends three pages discussing famous, decades-long disputes between the President and Congress—regarding congressional power to forbid the Presidential removal of executive officers, regarding the legislative veto, regarding congressional appointment of executive officers, and regarding the pocket veto—that would surely have been promptly resolved by a Congress-vs.-thePresident lawsuit if the impairment of a branch's powers alone conferred standing to commence litigation. But it does not, and never has; the "enormous power that the judiciary would acquire" from the ability to adjudicate such suits "would have made a mockery of [Hamilton's] quotation of Montesquieu to the effect that 'of the three powers above mentioned . . . the JUDICIARY is next to nothing.'" *Barnes* v. *Kline*, 759 F. 2d 21, 58 (CADC 1985) (Bork, J., dissenting) (quoting The Federalist No. 78 (A. Hamilton)).

To be sure, if Congress cannot invoke our authority in the way that JUSTICE ALITO proposes, then its only recourse is to confront the President directly. Unimaginable evil this is not. Our system is *designed* for confrontation. That is what "[a]mbition . . . counteract[ing] ambition," The Federalist, No. 51, at 322 (J. Madison), is all about. If majorities in both Houses of Congress care enough about the matter, they have available innumerable ways to compel executive action without a lawsuit—from refusing to confirm Presidential appointees to the elimination of funding. (Nothing says "enforce the Act" quite like ". . . or you will have money for little else.") But the condition is crucial; Congress must care enough to act against the President itself, not merely enough to instruct its lawyers to ask *us* to do so. Placing the Constitution's entirely anticipated political arm wrestling into permanent judicial receivership does not do the system a favor. And by the way, if the President loses the lawsuit but does not faithfully implement the Court's decree, just as he did not faithfully implement Congress's statute, what then? Only Congress can bring him to heel by . . . what do you think? Yes: a direct confrontation with the President.

II

For the reasons above, I think that this Court has, and the Court of Appeals had, no power to decide this suit. We should vacate the decision below and remand to the Court of Appeals for the Second Circuit, with instructions to dismiss the appeal. Given that the majority has volunteered its view of the merits, however, I proceed to discuss that as well.

A

There are many remarkable things about the majority's merits holding. The first is how rootless and shifting its justifications are. For example, the opinion starts with seven full pages about the traditional power of States to define domestic relations—initially fooling many readers, I am sure, into thinking that this is a federalism opinion. But we are eventually told that "it is unnecessary to decide whether this federal intrusion on state power is a violation of the Constitution," and that "[t]he State's power in defining the marital relation is of central relevance in this case quite apart from principles of federalism" be- cause "the State's decision to give this class of persons the right to marry conferred upon them a dignity and status of immense import." *Ante,* at 18. But no one questions the power of the States to define marriage (with the concomitant conferral of dignity and status), so what is the point of devoting seven pages to describing how long and well established that power is? Even after the opinion has formally disclaimed reliance upon principles of federalism, mentions of "the usual tradition of recognizing and accepting state definitions of marriage" continue. See, *e.g., ante,* at 20. What to make of this? The opinion never explains. My guess is that the majority, while reluctant to suggest that defining the meaning of "marriage" in federal statutes is unsupported by any of the Federal Government's enumerated powers,[4] nonetheless needs some rhetorical basis to support its pretense that today's prohibition of laws excluding same-sex marriage is confined to the Federal Government (leaving the second, state-law shoe to be dropped later, maybe next Term). But I am only guessing.

Equally perplexing are the opinion's references to "the Constitution's guarantee of equality." *Ibid.* Near the end of the opinion, we are told that although the "equal protection guarantee of the Fourteenth Amendment makes [the] Fifth Amendment [due process] right all the more specific and all the better understood and preserved"—what can *that* mean?—"the Fifth Amendment itself withdraws from Government the power to degrade or demean in the way this law does." *Ante,* at 25. The only possible interpretation of this statement is that the Equal Protection Clause, even the Equal Protection Clause as incorporated in the Due Process Clause, is not the basis for today's holding. But the portion of the majority opinion that explains why DOMA is unconstitutional (Part IV) begins by citing *Bolling* v. *Sharpe*, 347 U. S. 497 (1954), *Department of Agriculture* v. *Moreno*, 413 U. S. 528 (1973), and *Romer* v. *Evans*, 517 U. S. 620 (1996)—*all* of which are equal-protection cases.[5] And those three cases are the *only* authorities that the Court cites in Part IV about the Constitution's meaning, except for its citation of *Lawrence* v. *Texas*, 539 U. S. 558 (2003) (not an equal-protection case) to support its passing assertion that the Constitution protects the "moral and sexual choices" of same-sex couples, *ante,* at 23.

Moreover, if this is meant to be an equal-protection opinion, it is a confusing one. The opinion does not resolve and indeed does not even mention what had been the central question in this litigation: whether, under the Equal Protection Clause, laws restricting marriage to a man and a woman are reviewed for more than mere rationality. That is the issue that divided the parties and the court below, compare Brief for Respondent Bipartisan Legal Advisory Group of U. S. House of Representatives (merits) 24–28 (no), with Brief for Respondent Windsor (merits) 17–31 and Brief for United States (merits) 18–36 (yes); and compare 699 F. 3d 169, 180–185 (CA2 2012) (yes), with *id.,* at 208–211 (Straub, J., dissenting in part and concurring in part) (no). In accord with my previously expressed skepticism about the Court's "tiers of scrutiny" approach, I would review this classification only for its rationality.

See *United States* v. *Virginia*, 518 U. S. 515, 567–570 (1996) (SCALIA, J., dissenting). As nearly as I can tell, the Court agrees with that; its opinion does not apply strict scrutiny, and its central propositions are taken from rational-basis cases like *Moreno*. But the Court certainly does not *apply* anything that resembles that deferential framework. See *Heller* v. *Doe*, 509 U. S. 312, 320 (1993) (a classification "'must be upheld . . . if there is any reason- ably conceivable state of facts'" that could justify it).

The majority opinion need not get into the strict-vs.- rational-basis scrutiny question, and need not justify its holding under either, because it says that DOMA is unconstitutional as "a deprivation of the liberty of the person protected by the Fifth Amendment of the Constitution," *ante,* at 25; that it violates "basic due process" principles, *ante,* at 20; and that it inflicts an "injury and indignity" of a kind that denies "an essential part of the liberty protected by the Fifth Amendment," *ante,* at 19. The majority never utters the dread words "substantive due process," perhaps sensing the disrepute into which that doctrine has fallen, but that is what those statements mean. Yet the opinion does not argue that same-sex marriage is "deeply rooted in this Nation's history and tradition," *Washington* v. *Glucksberg*, 521 U. S. 702, 720–721 (1997), a claim that would of course be quite absurd. So would the further suggestion (also necessary, under our substantive-due-process precedents) that a world in which DOMA exists is one bereft of "'ordered liberty.'" *Id.,* at 721 (quoting *Palko* v. *Connecticut*, 302 U. S. 319, 325 (1937)).

Some might conclude that this loaf could have used a while longer in the oven. But that would be wrong; it is already overcooked. The most expert care in preparation cannot redeem a bad recipe. The sum of all the Court's nonspecific hand-waving is that this law is invalid (maybe on equal-protection grounds, maybe on substantive-dueprocess grounds, and perhaps with some amorphous federalism component playing a role) because it is motivated by a "'bare . . . desire to harm'" couples in same-sex marriages. *Ante,* at 20. It is this proposition with which I will therefore engage.

B

As I have observed before, the Constitution does not forbid the government to enforce traditional moral and sexual norms. See *Lawrence* v. *Texas*, 539 U. S. 558, 599 (2003) (SCALIA, J., dissenting). I will not swell the U. S. Reports with restatements of that point. It is enough to say that the Constitution neither requires nor forbids our society to approve of same-sex marriage, much as it neither requires nor forbids us to approve of no-fault divorce, polygamy, or the consumption of alcohol.

However, even setting aside traditional moral disapproval of same-sex marriage (or indeed same-sex sex), there are many perfectly valid—indeed, downright boring—justifying rationales for this legislation. Their existence ought to be the end of this case. For they give the lie to the Court's conclusion that only those with hateful hearts could have voted "aye" on this Act. And more importantly, they serve to make the contents of the legislators' hearts quite irrelevant: "It is a familiar principle of constitutional law that this Court will not strike down an otherwise constitutional statute on the basis of an alleged illicit legislative motive." *United States* v. *O'Brien*, 391 U. S. 367, 383 (1968). Or at least it *was* a familiar principle. By holding to the contrary, the majority has declared open season on any law that (in the opinion of the law's opponents and any panel of like-minded federal judges) can be characterized as mean-spirited.

The majority concludes that the only motive for this Act was the "bare . . . desire to harm a politically unpopular group." *Ante,* at 20. Bear in mind that the object of this condemnation is not the legislature of some once-Confederate Southern state (familiar objects of the Court's scorn, see, *e.g.*, *Edwards* v. *Aguillard*, 482 U. S. 578 (1987)), but our respected coordinate branches, the Congress and Presidency of the United States. Laying such a charge against them should require the most extraordinary evidence, and I would have thought that every attempt would be made to indulge a more anodyne explanation for the statute. The majority does the opposite—affirmatively concealing from the reader the arguments that exist in justification. It makes only a passing mention of the "arguments put forward" by the Act's defenders, and does not even trouble to paraphrase or describe them. See *ante,* at 21. I imagine that this is because it is harder to maintain the illusion of the Act's supporters as unhinged members of a wild-eyed lynch mob when one first describes their views as *they* see them.

To choose just one of these defenders' arguments, DOMA avoids difficult choice-of-law issues that will now arise absent a uniform federal definition of marriage. See, *e.g.,* Baude, Beyond DOMA: Choice of State Law in Fed- eral Statutes, 64 Stan. L. Rev. 1371 (2012). Imagine a pair of women who marry in Albany and then move to Alabama, which does not "recognize as valid any marriage of parties of the same sex." Ala. Code §30–1–19(e) (2011). When the couple files their next federal tax return, may it be a joint one? Which State's law controls, for federal-law purposes: their State of celebration (which recognizes the marriage) or their State of domicile (which does not)? (Does the answer depend on whether they were just visiting in Albany?) Are these questions to be answered as a matter of federal common law, or perhaps by borrowing a State's choice-of-law rules? If so, *which* State's? And what about States where the status of an out-of-state same-sex marriage is an unsettled question under local law? See *Godfrey* v. *Spano*, 13 N. Y. 3d 358, 920 N. E. 2d 328 (2009). DOMA avoided all of this uncertainty by specifying which marriages would be recognized for federal purposes. That is a classic purpose for a definitional provision.

Further, DOMA preserves the intended effects of prior legislation against then-unforeseen changes in circumstance. When Congress provided (for example) that a special estate-tax exemption would exist for spouses, this exemption reached only *opposite-sex* spouses—those being the only sort that were recognized in *any* State at the time of DOMA's passage. When it became clear that changes in state law might one day alter that balance, DOMA's definitional section was enacted to ensure that state-level experimentation did not automatically alter the basic operation of federal law, unless and until Congress made the further judgment to do so on its own. That is not animus—just stabilizing prudence. Congress has hardly demonstrated itself unwilling to make such further, revising judgments upon due deliberation. See, *e.g.,* Don't Ask, Don't Tell Repeal Act of 2010, 124 Stat. 3515.

The Court mentions none of this. Instead, it accuses the Congress that enacted this law and the President who signed it of something much worse than, for example, having acted in excess of enumerated federal powers—or even having drawn distinctions that prove to be irrational. Those legal errors may be made in good faith, errors though they are. But the majority says that the supporters of this Act acted with *malice*—with *the "purpose"* (*ante,* at 25) "to disparage and to injure" same-sex couples. It says that the motivation for DOMA was to "demean," *ibid.*; to "impose inequality," *ante,* at 22; to "impose . . . a stigma," *ante,* at 21; to deny people "equal dignity," *ibid.*; to brand gay people as "unworthy," *ante,* at 23; and to "*humiliat*[*e*]" their children, *ibid.* (emphasis added).

I am sure these accusations are quite untrue. To be sure (as the majority points out), the legislation is called the Defense of Marriage Act. But to defend traditional marriage is not to condemn, demean, or humiliate those who would prefer other arrangements, any more than to defend the Constitution of the United States is to condemn, demean, or humiliate other constitutions. To hurl such accusations so casually demeans *this institution*. In the majority's judgment, any resistance to its holding is beyond the pale of reasoned disagreement. To question its high-handed invalidation of a presumptively valid statute is to act (the majority is sure) with *the purpose* to "dis- parage," "injure," "degrade," "demean," and "humiliate" our fellow human beings, our fellow citizens, who are homosexual. All that, simply for supporting an Act that did no more than codify an aspect of marriage that had been unquestioned in our society for most of its existence— indeed, had been unquestioned in virtually all societies for virtually all of human history. It is one thing for a society to elect change; it is another for a court of law to impose change by adjudging those who oppose it *hostes humani generis*, enemies of the human race.

* * *

The penultimate sentence of the majority's opinion is a naked declaration that "[t]his opinion and its holding are confined" to those couples "joined in same-sex marriages made lawful by the State." *Ante,* at 26, 25. I have heard such "bald, unreasoned disclaimer[s]" before. *Lawrence*, 539 U. S., at 604. When the Court declared a constitutional right to homosexual sodomy, we were assured that the case had nothing, nothing at all to do with "whether the government must give formal recognition to any relationship that homosexual persons seek to enter." *Id.,* at 578. Now we are told that DOMA is invalid because it "demeans the couple, whose moral and sexual choices the Constitution protects," *ante,* at 23—with an accompanying citation of *Lawrence*. It takes real cheek for today's majority to assure us, as it is going out the door, that a constitutional requirement to give formal recognition to same-sex marriage is not at issue here—when what has preceded that assurance is a lecture on how superior the majority's moral judgment in favor of same-sex marriage is to the Congress's hateful moral judgment against it. I promise you this: The only thing that will "confine" the Court's holding is its sense of what it can get away with.

I do not mean to suggest disagreement with THE CHIEF JUSTICE's view, *ante,* p. 2–4 (dissenting opinion), that lower federal courts and state courts can distinguish today's case when the issue before them is state denial of marital status to same-sex couples—or even that this Court could *theoretically* do so. Lord, an opinion with such scatter-shot rationales as this one (federalism noises among them) can be distinguished in many ways. And deserves to be. State and lower federal courts should take the Court at its word and distinguish away.

In my opinion, however, the view that *this* Court will take of state prohibition of same-sex marriage is indicated beyond mistaking by today's opinion. As I have said, the real rationale of today's opinion, whatever disappearing trail of its legalistic argle-bargle one chooses to follow, is that DOMA is motivated by " 'bare . . . desire to harm'" couples in same-sex marriages. *Supra,* at 18. How easy it is, indeed how inevitable, to reach the same conclusion with regard to state laws denying same-sex couples marital status. Consider how easy (inevitable) it is to make the following substitutions in a passage from today's opinion *ante*, at 22:

> ~~"DOMA's~~ *This state law's* principal effect is to identify a subset of ~~state sanctioned marriages~~ *constitutionally protected sexual relationships,* see *Lawrence,* and make them unequal. The principal purpose is to impose inequality, not for other reasons like governmental efficiency. Responsibilities, as well as rights, enhance the dignity and integrity of the person. And ~~DOMA~~ *this state law* contrives to deprive some couples ~~married under the laws of their State~~ *enjoying constitutionally protected sexual relationships*, but not other couples, of both rights and responsibilities."

Or try this passage, from *ante*, at 22–23:

> ~~"[DOMA]~~ *This state law* tells those couples, and all the world, that their otherwise valid ~~marriages~~ *relationships* are unworthy of ~~federal~~ *state* recognition. This places same-sex couples in an unstable position of being in a second-tier ~~marriage~~ *relationship.* The differentiation demeans the couple, whose moral and sexual choices the Constitution protects, see *Lawrence*, ..."

Or this, from *ante*, at 23—which does not even require alteration, except as to the invented number:

> "And it humiliates ~~tens of~~ thousands of children now being raised by same-sex couples. The law in question makes it even more difficult for the children to understand the integrity and closeness of their own family and its concord with other families in their commu- nity and in their daily lives."

Similarly transposable passages—deliberately transpos- able, I think—abound. In sum, that Court which finds it so horrific that Congress irrationally and hatefully robbed same-sex couples of the "personhood and dignity" which state legislatures conferred upon them, will of a certitude be similarly appalled by state legislatures' irrational and hateful failure to acknowledge that "personhood and dig- nity" in the first place. *Ante*, at 26. As far as this Court is concerned, no one should be fooled; it is just a matter of listening and waiting for the other shoe.

By formally declaring anyone opposed to same-sex marriage an enemy of human decency, the majority arms well every challenger to a state law restricting marriage to its traditional definition. Henceforth those challengers will lead with this Court's declaration that there is "no legitimate purpose" served by such a law, and will claim that the traditional definition has "the purpose and effect to disparage and to injure" the "personhood and dignity" of same-sex couples, see *ante,* at 25, 26. The majority's limiting assurance will be meaningless in the face of language like that, as the majority well knows. That is why the language is there. The result will be a judicial distortion of our society's debate over marriage—a debate that can seem in need of our clumsy "help" only to a member of this institution.

As to that debate: Few public controversies touch an institution so central to the lives of so many, and few inspire such attendant passion by good people on all sides. Few public controversies will ever demonstrate so vividly the beauty of what our Framers gave us, a gift the Court pawns today to buy its stolen moment in the spotlight: a system of government that permits us to rule *ourselves*. Since DOMA's passage, citizens on all sides of the question have seen victories and they have seen defeats. There have been plebiscites, legislation, persuasion, and loud voices—in other words, democracy. Victories in one place for some, see North Carolina Const., Amdt. 1 (providing that "[m]arriage between one man and one woman is the only domestic legal union that shall be valid or recognized in this State") (approved by a popular vote, 61% to 39% on May 8, 2012),[6] are offset by victories in other places for others, see Maryland Question 6 (establishing "that Maryland's civil marriage laws allow gay and lesbian couples to obtain a civil marriage license") (approved by a popular vote, 52% to 48%, on November 6, 2012).[7] Even in a *single State*, the question has come out differently on different occasions. Compare Maine Question 1 (permitting "the State of Maine to issue marriage licenses to same-sex couples") (approved by a popular vote, 53% to 47%, on November 6, 2012)[8] with Maine Question 1 (rejecting "the new law that lets same-sex couples marry") (approved by a popular vote, 53% to 47%, on November 3, 2009).[9]

In the majority's telling, this story is black-and-white: Hate your neighbor or come along with us. The truth is more complicated. It is hard to admit that one's political opponents are not monsters, especially in a struggle like this one, and the challenge in the end proves more than today's Court can handle. Too bad. A reminder that disagreement over something so fundamental as marriage can still be politically legitimate would have been a fit task for what in earlier times was called the judicial temperament. We might have covered ourselves with honor today, by promising all sides of this debate that it was theirs to settle and that we would respect their resolution. We might have let the People decide.

But that the majority will not do. Some will rejoice in today's decision, and some will despair at it; that is the nature of a controversy that matters so much to so many. But the Court has cheated both sides, robbing the winners of an honest victory, and the losers of the peace that comes from a fair defeat. We owed both of them better. I dissent.

ALITO, J., dissenting

SUPREME COURT OF THE UNITED STATES

No. 12–307

UNITED STATES, PETITIONER *v.* EDITH SCHLAIN WINDSOR, IN HER CAPACITY AS EXECUTOR OF THE ESTATE OF THEA CLARA SPYER, ET AL.

ON WRIT OF CERTIORARI TO THE UNITED STATES COURT OF APPEALS FOR THE SECOND CIRCUIT

[June 26, 2013]

JUSTICE ALITO, with whom JUSTICE THOMAS joins as to Parts II and III, dissenting.

Our Nation is engaged in a heated debate about same-sex marriage. That debate is, at bottom, about the nature of the institution of marriage. Respondent Edith Windsor, supported by the United States, asks this Court to intervene in that debate, and although she couches her argument in different terms, what she seeks is a holding that enshrines in the Constitution a particular understanding of marriage under which the sex of the partners makes no difference. The Constitution, however, does not dictate that choice. It leaves the choice to the people, acting through their elected representatives at both the federal and state levels. I would therefore hold that Congress did not violate Windsor's constitutional rights by enacting §3 of the Defense of Marriage Act (DOMA), 110 Stat. 2419, which defines the meaning of marriage under federal statutes that either confer upon married persons certain federal benefits or impose upon them certain federal obligations.

I

I turn first to the question of standing. In my view, the United States clearly is not a proper petitioner in this case. The United States does not ask us to overturn the judgment of the court below or to alter that judgment in any way. Quite to the contrary, the United States argues emphatically in favor of the correctness of that judgment. We have never before reviewed a decision at the sole behest of a party that took such a position, and to do so would be to render an advisory opinion, in violation of Article III's dictates. For the reasons given in JUSTICE SCALIA's dissent, I do not find the Court's arguments to the contrary to be persuasive.

Whether the Bipartisan Legal Advisory Group of the House of Representatives (BLAG) has standing to petition is a much more difficult question. It is also a signifi- cantly closer question than whether the intervenors in *Hollingsworth* v. *Perry*, *ante,* p.___—which the Court also decides today—have standing to appeal. It is remarkable that the Court has simultaneously decided that the United States, which "receive[d] all that [it] ha[d] sought" below, *Deposit Guaranty Nat. Bank* v. *Roper*, 445 U. S. 326, 333 (1980), is a proper petitioner in this case but that the intervenors in *Hollingsworth*, who represent the party that lost in the lower court, are not. In my view, both the *Hollingsworth* intervenors and BLAG have standing.[1]

A party invoking the Court's authority has a sufficient stake to permit it to appeal when it has "'suffered an injury in fact' that is caused by 'the conduct complained of ' and that 'will be redressed by a favorable decision.'" *Camreta* v. *Greene*, 563 U. S. ___, ___ (2011) (slip op., at 5) (quoting *Lujan* v. *Defenders of Wildlife*, 504 U. S. 555, 560–561 (1992)). In the present case, the House of Representatives, which has authorized BLAG to represent its interests in this matter,[2] suffered just such an injury.

In *INS* v. *Chadha*, 462 U. S. 919 (1983), the Court held that the two Houses of Congress were "proper parties" to file a petition in defense of the constitutionality of the one-house veto statute, *id.*, at 930, n. 5 (internal quotation marks omitted). Accordingly, the Court granted and decided petitions by both the Senate and the House, in addition to the Executive's petition. *Id.*, at 919, n.*. That the two Houses had standing to petition is not surprising: The Court of Appeals' decision in *Chadha*, by holding the one-house veto to be unconstitutional, had limited Congress' power to legislate. In discussing Article III standing, the Court suggested that Congress suffered a similar injury whenever federal legislation it had passed was struck down, noting that it had "long held that Congress is the proper party to defend the validity of a statute when an agency of government, as a defendant charged with enforcing the statute, agrees with plaintiffs that the statute is inapplicable or unconstitutional." *Id.*, at 940.

The United States attempts to distinguish *Chadha* on the ground that it "involved an unusual statute that vested the House and the Senate themselves each with special procedural rights—namely, the right effectively to veto Executive action." Brief for United States (jurisdiction) 36. But that is a distinction without a difference: just as the Court of Appeals decision that the *Chadha* Court affirmed impaired Congress' power by striking down the one-house veto, so the Second Circuit's decision here impairs Congress' legislative power by striking down an Act of Congress. The United States has not explained why the fact that the impairment at issue in *Chadha* was "special" or "procedural" has any relevance to whether Congress suffered an injury. Indeed, because legislating is Congress' central function, any impairment of that function is a more grievous injury than the impairment of a procedural add-on.

The Court's decision in *Coleman* v. *Miller*, 307 U. S. 433 (1939), bolsters this conclusion. In *Coleman*, we held that a group of state senators had standing to challenge a lower court decision approving the procedures used to ratify an amendment to the Federal Constitution. We reasoned that the senators' votes—which would otherwise have carried the day—were nullified by that action. See *id.,* at 438 ("Here, the plaintiffs include twenty senators, whose votes against ratification have been overridden and virtually held for naught although if they are right in their contentions their votes would have been sufficient to defeat ratification. We think that these senators have a plain, direct and adequate interest in maintaining the effectiveness of their votes"); *id.*, at 446 ("[W]e find no departure from principle in recognizing in the instant case that at least the twenty senators whose votes, if their contention were sustained, would have been sufficient to defeat the resolution ratifying the proposed constitutional amendment, have an interest in the controversy which, treated by the state court as a basis for entertaining and deciding the federal questions, is sufficient to give the Court jurisdiction to review that decision"). By striking down §3 of DOMA as unconstitutional, the Second Circuit effectively "held for naught" an Act of Congress. Just as the state-senator-petitioners in *Coleman* were necessary parties to the amendment's ratification, the House of Representatives was a necessary party to DOMA's passage; indeed, the House's vote would have been sufficient to prevent DOMA's repeal if the Court had not chosen to execute that repeal judicially.

Both the United States and the Court-appointed *amicus* err in arguing that *Raines* v. *Byrd*, 521 U. S. 811 (1997), is to the contrary. In that case, the Court held that Members of Congress who had voted "nay" to the Line Item Veto Act did not have standing to challenge that statute in federal court. *Raines* is inapposite for two reasons. First, *Raines* dealt with individual Members of Congress and specifically pointed to the individual Members' lack of institutional endorsement as a sign of their standing problem: "We attach some importance to the fact that appellees have not been authorized to represent their respective Houses of Congress in this action, and indeed both Houses actively oppose their suit." *Id.*, at 829; see also *ibid.*, n.10 (citing cases to the effect that "members of collegial bodies do not have standing to perfect an appeal the body itself has declined to take" (internal quotation marks omitted)).

Second, the Members in *Raines*—unlike the state senators in *Coleman*—were not the pivotal figures whose votes would have caused the Act to fail absent some challenged action. Indeed, it is telling that *Raines* characterized *Coleman* as standing "for the proposition that legislators whose votes would have been sufficient to defeat (or enact) a specific legislative Act have standing to sue if that legislative action goes into effect (or does not go into effect), on the ground that their votes have been completely nullified." 521 U. S., at 823. Here, by contrast, passage by the House was needed for DOMA to become law. U. S. Const., Art. I, §7 (bicameralism and presentment requirements for legislation).

I appreciate the argument that the Constitution confers on the President alone the authority to defend federal law in litigation, but in my view, as I have explained, that argument is contrary to the Court's holding in *Chadha*, and it is certainly contrary to the *Chadha* Court's endorsement of the principle that "Congress is the proper party to defend the validity of a statute" when the Executive refuses to do so on constitutional grounds. 462 U. S., at 940. See also 2 U. S. C. §288h(7) (Senate Legal Counsel shall defend the constitutionality of Acts of Congress when placed in issue).[3] Accordingly, in the narrow category of cases in which a court strikes down an Act of Congress and the Executive declines to defend the Act, Congress both has standing to defend the undefended statute and is a proper party to do so.

II

Windsor and the United States argue that §3 of DOMA violates the equal protection principles that the Court has found in the Fifth Amendment's Due Process Clause. See Brief for Respondent Windsor (merits) 17–62; Brief for United States (merits) 16–54; cf. *Bolling* v. *Sharpe*, 347 U. S. 497 (1954). The Court rests its holding on related arguments. See *ante*, at 24–25.

Same-sex marriage presents a highly emotional and important question of public policy—but not a difficult question of constitutional law. The Constitution does not guarantee the right to enter into a same-sex marriage. Indeed, no provision of the Constitution speaks to the issue.

The Court has sometimes found the Due Process Clauses to have a substantive component that guarantees liber- ties beyond the absence of physical restraint. And the Court's holding that "DOMA is unconstitutional as a dep- rivation of the liberty of the person protected by the Fifth Amendment of the Constitution," *ante*, at 25, suggests that substantive due process may partially underlie the Court's decision today. But it is well established that any "substantive" component to the Due Process Clause protects only "those fundamental rights and lib- erties which are, objectively, 'deeply rooted in this Nation's history and tradition,'" *Washington* v. *Glucksberg*, 521 U. S. 702, 720–721 (1997); *Snyder* v. *Massachusetts*, 291 U. S. 97, 105 (1934) (referring to fundamental rights as those that are so "rooted in the traditions and conscience of our people as to be ranked as fundamental"), as well as "'implicit in the concept of ordered liberty,' such that 'neither liberty nor justice would exist if they were sacrificed.'" *Glucksberg*, *supra*, at 721 (quoting *Palko* v. *Connecticut*, 302 U. S. 319, 325–326 (1937)).

It is beyond dispute that the right to same-sex marriage is not deeply rooted in this Nation's history and tradition. In this country, no State permitted same-sex marriage until the Massachusetts Supreme Judicial Court held in 2003 that limiting marriage to opposite-sex couples violated the State Constitution. See *Goodridge* v. *Department of Public Health*, 440 Mass. 309, 798 N. E. 2d 941. Nor is the right to same-sex marriage deeply rooted in the traditions of other nations. No country allowed same-sex couples to marry until the Netherlands did so in 2000.[4]

What Windsor and the United States seek, therefore, is not the protection of a deeply rooted right but the recognition of a very new right, and they seek this innovation not from a legislative body elected by the people, but from unelected judges. Faced with such a request, judges have cause for both caution and humility.

The family is an ancient and universal human institution. Family structure reflects the characteristics of a civilization, and changes in family structure and in the popular understanding of marriage and the family can have profound effects. Past changes in the understanding of marriage—for example, the gradual ascendance of the idea that romantic love is a prerequisite to marriage— have had far-reaching consequences. But the process by which such consequences come about is complex, involving the interaction of numerous factors, and tends to occur over an extended period of time.

We can expect something similar to take place if same-sex marriage becomes widely accepted. The long-term consequences of this change are not now known and are unlikely to be ascertainable for some time to come.[5] There are those who think that allowing same-sex marriage will seriously undermine the institution of marriage. See, *e.g.,* S. Girgis, R. Anderson, & R. George, What is Marriage? Man and Woman: A Defense 53–58 (2012); Finnis, Marriage: A Basic and Exigent Good, 91 The Monist 388, 398 (2008).[6] Others think that recognition of same-sex marriage will fortify a now-shaky institution. See, *e.g.,* A. Sullivan, Virtually Normal: An Argument About Homosexuality 202–203 (1996); J. Rauch, Gay Marriage: Why It Is Good for Gays, Good for Straights, and Good for Amer- ica 94 (2004).

At present, no one—including social scientists, philosophers, and historians—can predict with any certainty what the long-term ramifications of widespread acceptance of same-sex marriage will be. And judges are certainly not equipped to make such an assessment. The Members of this Court have the authority and the responsibility to interpret and apply the Constitution. Thus, if the Constitution contained a provision guaranteeing the right to marry a person of the same sex, it would be our duty to enforce that right. But the Constitution simply does not speak to the issue of same-sex marriage. In our system of government, ultimate sovereignty rests with the people, and the people have the right to control their own destiny. Any change on a question so fundamental should be made by the people through their elected officials.

III

Perhaps because they cannot show that same-sex marriage is a fundamental right under our Constitution, Windsor and the United States couch their arguments in equal protection terms. They argue that §3 of DOMA discriminates on the basis of sexual orientation, that classifications based on sexual orientation should trigger a form of "heightened" scrutiny, and that §3 cannot survive such scrutiny. They further maintain that the governmental interests that §3 purports to serve are not sufficiently important and that it has not been adequately shown that §3 serves those interests very well. The Court's holding, too, seems to rest on "the equal protection guarantee of the Fourteenth Amendment," *ante,* at 25— although the Court is careful not to adopt most of Windsor's and the United States' argument.

In my view, the approach that Windsor and the United States advocate is misguided. Our equal protection frame- work, upon which Windsor and the United States rely, is a judicial construct that provides a useful mechanism for analyzing a certain universe of equal protection cases. But that framework is ill suited for use in evaluating the constitutionality of laws based on the traditional understanding of marriage, which fundamentally turn on what marriage is.

Underlying our equal protection jurisprudence is the central notion that "[a] classification 'must be reasonable, not arbitrary, and must rest upon some ground of difference having a fair and substantial relation to the object of the legislation, so that all persons similarly circumstanced shall be treated alike.'" *Reed* v. *Reed*, 404 U. S. 71, 76 (1971) (quoting *F. S. Royter Guano Co.* v. *Virginia*, 253 U. S. 412, 415 (1920)). The modern tiers of scrutiny—on which Windsor and the United States rely so heavily—are a heuristic to help judges determine when classifications have that "fair and substantial relation to the object of the legislation." *Reed, supra,* at 76.

So, for example, those classifications subject to strict scrutiny—*i.e.,* classifications that must be "narrowly tailored" to achieve a "compelling" government interest, *Parents Involved in Community Schools* v. *Seattle School Dist. No. 1*, 551 U. S. 701, 720 (2007) (internal quotation marks omitted)—are those that are "so seldom relevant to the achievement of any legitimate state interest that laws grounded in such considerations are deemed to reflect prejudice and antipathy." *Cleburne* v. *Cleburne Living Center, Inc.*, 473 U. S. 432, 440 (1985); cf. *id.*, at 452–453 (Stevens, J., concurring) ("It would be utterly irrational to limit the franchise on the basis of height or weight; it is equally invalid to limit it on the basis of skin color. None of these attributes has any bearing at all on the citizen's willingness or ability to exercise that civil right").

In contrast, those characteristics subject to so-called intermediate scrutiny—*i.e.,* those classifications that must be "'substantially related'" to the achievement of "important governmental objective[s]," *United States* v. *Virginia*, 518 U. S. 515, 524 (1996); *id.,* at 567 (SCALIA, J., dissenting)—are those that are *sometimes* relevant considerations to be taken into account by legislators, but "generally provid[e] no sensible ground for different treatment," *Cleburne*, *supra*, at 440. For example, the Court has held that statutory rape laws that criminalize sexual intercourse with a woman under the age of 18 years, but place no similar liability on partners of underage men, are grounded in the very real distinction that "young men and young women are not similarly situated with respect to the problems and the risks of sexual intercourse." *Michael M.* v. *Superior Court, Sonoma Cty.*, 450 U. S. 464, 471 (1981) (plurality opnion). The plurality reasoned that "[o]nly women may become pregnant, and they suffer disproportionately the profound physical, emotional, and psychological consequences of sexual activity." *Ibid.* In other contexts, however, the Court has found that classifications based on gender are "arbitrary," *Reed*, *supra*, at 76, and based on "outmoded notions of the relative capabilities of men and women," *Cleburne*, *supra*, at 441, as when a State provides that a man must always be preferred to an equally qualified woman when both seek to administer the estate of a deceased party, see *Reed*, *supra*, at 76–77.

Finally, so-called rational-basis review applies to classifications based on "distinguishing characteristics relevant to interests the State has the authority to implement." *Cleburne*, *supra*, at 441. We have long recognized that "the equal protection of the laws must coexist with the practical necessity that most legislation classifies for one purpose or another, with resulting disadvantages to various groups or persons." *Romer* v. *Evans*, 517 U. S. 620, 631 (1996). As a result, in rational-basis cases, where the court does not view the classification at issue as "inher- ently suspect," *Adarand Constructors, Inc.* v. *Peña*, 515 U. S. 200, 218 (1995) (internal quotation marks omitted), "the courts have been very reluctant, as they should be in our federal system and with our respect for the separation of powers, to closely scrutinize legislative choices as to whether, how, and to what extent those interests should be pursued." *Cleburne*, *supra*, at 441–442.

In asking the Court to determine that §3 of DOMA is subject to and violates heightened scrutiny, Windsor and the United States thus ask us to rule that the presence of two members of the opposite sex is as rationally related to marriage as white skin is to voting or a Y-chromosome is to the ability to administer an estate. That is a striking request and one that unelected judges should pause before granting. Acceptance of the argument would cast all those who cling to traditional beliefs about the nature of marriage in the role of bigots or superstitious fools.

By asking the Court to strike down DOMA as not satisfying some form of heightened scrutiny, Windsor and the United States are really seeking to have the Court resolve a debate between two competing views of marriage.

The first and older view, which I will call the "traditional" or "conjugal" view, sees marriage as an intrinsically opposite-sex institution. BLAG notes that virtually every culture, including many not influenced by the Abrahamic religions, has limited marriage to people of the opposite sex. Brief for Respondent BLAG (merits) 2 (citing *Hernandez* v. *Robles*, 7 N. Y. 3d 338, 361, 855 N. E. 2d 1, 8 (2006) ("Until a few decades ago, it was an accepted truth for almost everyone who ever lived, in any society in which marriage existed, that there could be marriages only between participants of different sex")). And BLAG attempts to explain this phenomenon by arguing that the institution of marriage was created for the purpose of channeling heterosexual intercourse into a structure that supports child rearing. Brief for Respondent BLAG 44–46, 49. Others explain the basis for the institution in more philosophical terms. They argue that marriage is essentially the solemnizing of a comprehensive, exclusive, permanent union that is intrinsically ordered to producing new life, even if it does not always do so. See, *e.g.*, Girgis, Anderson, & George, What is Marriage? Man and Woman: A Defense, at 23–28. While modern cultural changes have weakened the link between marriage and procreation in the popular mind, there is no doubt that, throughout human history and across many cultures, marriage has been viewed as an exclusively opposite-sex institution and as one inextricably linked to procreation and biological kinship.

The other, newer view is what I will call the "consent-based" vision of marriage, a vision that primarily defines marriage as the solemnization of mutual commitment— marked by strong emotional attachment and sexual attraction—between two persons. At least as it applies to heterosexual couples, this view of marriage now plays a very prominent role in the popular understanding of the institution. Indeed, our popular culture is infused with this understanding of marriage. Proponents of same-sex marriage argue that because gender differentiation is not relevant to this vision, the exclusion of same-sex couples from the institution of marriage is rank discrimination.

The Constitution does not codify either of these views of marriage (although I suspect it would have been hard at the time of the adoption of the Constitution or the Fifth Amendment to find Americans who did not take the traditional view for granted). The silence of the Constitution on this question should be enough to end the matter as far as the judiciary is concerned. Yet, Windsor and the United States implicitly ask us to endorse the consent-based view of marriage and to reject the traditional view, thereby arrogating to ourselves the power to decide a question that philosophers, historians, social scientists, and theologians are better qualified to explore.[7] Because our constitutional order assigns the resolution of questions of this nature to the people, I would not presume to en- shrine either vision of marriage in our constitutional jurisprudence.

Legislatures, however, have little choice but to decide between the two views. We have long made clear that neither the political branches of the Federal Government nor state governments are required to be neutral between competing visions of the good, provided that the vision of the good that they adopt is not countermanded by the Constitution. See, *e.g., Rust* v. *Sullivan*, 500 U. S. 173, 192 (1991) ("[T]he government 'may make a value judgment favoring childbirth over abortion'" (quoting *Maher* v. *Rue*, 432 U. S. 464, 474 (1977))). Accordingly, both Congress and the States are entitled to enact laws recognizing either of the two understandings of marriage. And given the size of government and the degree to which it now regulates daily life, it seems unlikely that either Congress or the States could maintain complete neutrality even if they tried assiduously to do so.

Rather than fully embracing the arguments made by Windsor and the United States, the Court strikes down §3 of DOMA as a classification not properly supported by its objectives. The Court reaches this conclusion in part because it believes that §3 encroaches upon the States' sovereign prerogative to define marriage. See *ante,* at 21– 22 ("As the title and dynamics of the bill indicate, its purpose is to discourage enactment of state same-sex marriage laws and to restrict the freedom and choice of couples married under those laws if they are enacted. The congressional goal was 'to put a thumb on the scales and influence a state's decision as to how to shape its own marriage laws'" (quoting *Massachusetts* v. *United States Dept. of Health and Human Servs.*, 682 F. 3d 1, 12–13 (CA1 2012))). Indeed, the Court's ultimate conclusion is that DOMA falls afoul of the Fifth Amendment because it "singles out a class of persons deemed *by a State* entitled to recognition and protection to enhance their own liberty" and "imposes a disability on the class by refusing to acknowledge a status *the State finds* to be dignified and proper." *Ante*, at 25 (emphasis added).

To the extent that the Court takes the position that the question of same-sex marriage should be resolved primarily at the state level, I wholeheartedly agree. I hope that the Court will ultimately permit the people of each State to decide this question for themselves. Unless the Court is willing to allow this to occur, the whiffs of federalism in the today's opinion of the Court will soon be scattered to the wind.

In any event, §3 of DOMA, in my view, does not encroach on the prerogatives of the States, assuming of course that the many federal statutes affected by DOMA have not already done so. Section 3 does not prevent any State from recognizing same-sex marriage or from extending to same-sex couples any right, privilege, benefit, or obligation stemming from state law. All that §3 does is to define a class of persons to whom federal law extends certain special benefits and upon whom federal law imposes certain special burdens. In these provisions, Congress used marital status as a way of defining this class—in part, I assume, because it viewed marriage as a valua- ble institution to be fostered and in part because it viewed married couples as comprising a unique type of economic unit that merits special regulatory treatment. Assuming that Congress has the power under the Constitution to enact the laws affected by §3, Congress has the power to define the category of persons to whom those laws apply.

* * *

For these reasons, I would hold that §3 of DOMA does not violate the Fifth Amendment. I respectfully dissent.

End Notes for SCALIA, J., dissenting

[1] For an even more advanced scavenger hunt, one might search the annals of Anglo-American law for another "Motion to Dismiss" like the one the United States filed in District Court: It argued that the court should agree "with Plaintiff and the United States" and "*not* dismiss" the complaint. (Emphasis mine.) Then, having gotten exactly what it asked for, the United States promptly appealed.

[2] There the Justice Department's refusal to defend the legislation was in accord with its longstanding (and entirely reasonable) practice of declining to defend legislation that in its view infringes upon Presidential powers. There is no justification for the Justice Department's abandoning the law in the present case. The majority opinion makes a point of scolding the President for his "failure to defend the constitutionality of an Act of Congress based on a constitutional theory not yet established in judicial decisions," *ante,* at 12. But the rebuke is tongue-in-cheek, for the majority gladly gives the President what he wants. Contrary to all precedent, it decides this case (and even decides it the way the President wishes) *despite* his abandonment of the defense and the consequent absence of a case or controversy.

[3] JUSTICE ALITO attempts to limit his argument by claiming that Congress is injured (and can therefore appeal) when its statute is held unconstitutional without Presidential defense, but is *not* injured when its statute is held unconstitutional *despite* Presidential defense. I do not understand that line. The injury to Congress is the same whether the President has defended the statute or not. And if the injury is threatened, why should Congress not be able to participate in the suit from the beginning, just as the President can? And if having a statute declared unconstitutional (and therefore inoperative) by a court is an injury, why is it not an

injury when a statute is declared unconstitutional by the President and rendered inoperative by his consequent failure to enforce it? Or when the President simply declines to enforce it without opining on its constitutionality? If it is the *inoperativeness* that constitutes the injury—the "impairment of [the legislative] function," as JUSTICE ALITO puts it, *post,* at 4—it should make no difference which of the other two branches inflicts it, and whether the Constitution is the pretext. A principled and predictable system of jurisprudence cannot rest upon a shifting concept of injury, designed to support standing when we would like it. If this Court agreed with JUSTICE ALITO's distinction, its opinion in *Raines* v. *Byrd*, 521 U. S. 811 (1997), which involved an original suit by Members of Congress challenging an assertedly unconstitutional law, would have been written quite differently; and JUSTICE ALITO's distinguishing of that case on grounds quite irrelevant to his theory of standing would have been unnecessary.

[4] Such a suggestion would be impossible, given the Federal Government's long history of making pronouncements regarding marriage—for example, conditioning Utah's entry into the Union upon its prohibition of polygamy. See Act of July 16, 1894, ch. 138, §3, 28 Stat. 108 ("The constitution [of Utah]" must provide "perfect toleration of religious sentiment," "*Provided*, That polygamous or plural marriages are forever prohibited").

[5] Since the Equal Protection Clause technically applies only against the States, see U. S. Const., Amdt. 14, *Bolling* and *Moreno*, dealing with federal action, relied upon "the equal protection component of the Due Process Clause of the Fifth Amendment," *Moreno*, 413 U. S., at 533.

[6] North Carolina State Board of Elections, Official Results: Primary Election of May 8, 2012, Constitutional Amendment.

[7] Maryland State Board of Elections, Official 2012 Presidential General Election Results for All State Questions, Question 06.

[8] Maine Bureau of Elections, Nov. 3, 2009, Referendum Tabulation (Question 1).

[9] Maine Bureau of Elections, Nov. 6, 2012, Referendum Election Tabulations (Question 1).

End Notes for ALITO, J., dissenting

[1] Our precedents make clear that, in order to support our jurisdiction, BLAG must demonstrate that it had Article III standing in its own right, quite apart from its status as an intervenor. See *Diamond* v. *Charles*, 476 U. S. 54, 68 (1986) ("Although intervenors are considered parties entitled, among other things, to seek review by this Court, an intervenor's right to continue a suit in the absence of the party on whose side intervention was permitted is contingent upon a showing by the intervenor that he fulfills the requirements of Art. III" (citation omitted)); *Arizonans for Official English* v. *Arizona*, 520 U. S. 43, 64 (1997) ("Standing to defend on appeal in the place of an original defendant, no less than standing to sue, demands that the litigant possess a direct stake in the outcome" (internal quotation marks omitted)); *id.*, at 65 ("An intervenor cannot step into the shoes of the original party unless the intervenor independently fulfills the requirements of Article III" (internal quotation marks omitted)).

[2] H. Res. 5, 113th Cong., 1st Sess., §4(a)(1)(B) (2013) ("[BLAG] continues to speak for, and articulates the institutional position of, the House in all litigation matters in which it appears, including in Windsor v. United States").

[3] *Buckley* v. *Valeo*, 424 U. S. 1 (1976), is not to the contrary. The Court's statements there concerned enforcement, not defense.

[4] Curry-Sumner, A Patchwork of Partnerships: Comparative Overview of Registration Schemes in Europe, in Legal Recognition of Same-Sex Partnerships 71, 72 (K. Boele-Woelki & A. Fuchs eds., rev. 2d ed., 2012).

[5] As sociologists have documented, it sometimes takes decades to document the effects of social changes—like the sharp rise in divorce rates following the advent of no-fault divorce—on children and society. See generally J. Wallerstein, J. Lewis, & S. Blakeslee, The Unexpected Legacy of Divorce: The 25 Year Landmark Study (2000).

[6] Among those holding that position, some deplore and some applaud this predicted development. Compare, *e.g.,* Wardle, "Multiply and Replenish": Considering Same-Sex Marriage in Light of State Interests in Marital Procreation, 24 Harv. J. L. & Pub. Pol'y 771, 799 (2001) ("Culturally, the legalization of same-sex marriage would send a message that would undermine the social boundaries relating to marriage and family relations. The confusion of social roles linked with marriage and parenting would be tremendous, and the message of 'anything goes' in the way of sexual behavior, procreation, and parenthood would wreak its greatest havoc among groups of vulnerable individuals who most need the encouragement of bright line laws and clear social mores concerning procreative responsibility") and Gallagher, (How) Will Gay Marriage Weaken Marriage as a Social Institution: A Reply to Andrew Koppelman, 2 U. St. Thomas L. J. 33, 58 (2005) ("If the idea of marriage really does matter—if society really does need a social institution that manages opposite-sex attractions in the interests of children and society—then taking an already weakened social institution, subjecting it to radical new redefinitions, and hoping that there are no consequences is probably neither a wise nor a compassionate idea"), with Brownworth, Something Borrowed, Something Blue: Is Marriage Right for Queers? in I Do/I Don't: Queers on Marriage 53, 58– 59 (G. Wharton & I. Phillips eds. 2004) (Former President George W. "Bush is correct . . . when he states that allowing same-sex couples to marry will weaken the institution of marriage. It most certainly will do so, and that will make marriage a far better concept than it previously has been") and Willis, Can Marriage Be Saved? A Forum, The Nation, p. 16 (2004) (celebrating the fact that "conferring the legitimacy of marriage on homosexual relations will introduce an implicit revolt against the institution into its very heart").

[7] The degree to which this question is intractable to typical judicial processes of decisionmaking was highlighted by the trial in *Hollingsworth* v. *Perry, ante,* p. ___. In that case, the trial judge, after receiving testimony from some expert witnesses, purported to make "findings of fact" on such questions as why marriage came to be, *Perry* v. *Schwarzenegger,* 704 F. Supp. 2d 921, 958 (ND Cal. 2010) (finding of fact no. 27) ("Marriage between a man and a woman was traditionally organized based on presumptions of division of labor along gender lines. Men were seen as suited for certain types of work and women for others. Women were seen as suited to raise children and men were seen as suited to provide for the family"), what marriage is, *id.*, at 961 (finding of fact no. 34) ("Marriage is the state recognition and approval of a couple's choice to live with each other, to remain committed to one another and to form a household based on their own feelings about one another and to join in an economic partnership and support one another and any dependents"), and the effect legalizing same-sex marriage would have on opposite-sex marriage, *id.*, at 972 (finding of fact no. 55) ("Permitting same-sex couples to marry will not affect the number of opposite-sex couples who marry, divorce, cohabit, have children outside of marriage or otherwise affect the stability of opposite-sex marriages").

At times, the trial reached the heights of parody, as when the trial judge questioned his ability to take into account the views of great thinkers of the past because they were unavailable to testify in person in his courtroom. See 13 Tr. in No. C 09–2292 VRW (ND Cal.), pp. 3038–3039.

And, if this spectacle were not enough, some professors of constitutional law have argued that we are bound to accept the trial judge's findings—including those on major philosophical questions and predictions about the future—unless they are "clearly erroneous." See Brief for Constitutional Law and Civil Procedure Professors as *Amici Curiae* in *Hollingsworth* v. *Perry*, O. T. 2012, No. 12–144, pp. 2–3 ("[T]he district court's factual findings are compelling and should be given significant weight"); *id.*, at 25 ("Under any standard of review, this Court should credit and adopt the trial court's findings because they result from rigorous and exacting application of the Federal Rules of Evidence, and are supported by reliable research and by the unanimous consensus of mainstream social science experts"). Only an arrogant legal culture that has lost all appreciation of its own limitations could take such a suggestion seriously.

Index

D

E

F

G

H

I

J

K

L

M

N

O

P

R

S

T

U

V

W

Y